Criminal Justice

Prentice Hall's Reality Reading Series

Criminal Justice
A Collection
of True-Crime Cases

RON GRIMMING
Director, Miami Dade College, School of Justice
Director of the Florida Highway Patrol (Retired)
Deputy Director of the Illinois State Police (Retired)

DEBBIE J. GOODMAN, M.S.
Chairperson, Miami Dade College School of Justice

PEARSON
Prentice
Hall

Upper Saddle River, New Jersey 07458

Library of Congress Cataloging-in-Publication Data

Grimming, Ron.
  Criminal justice : a collection of true-crime cases / Ron Grimming, Debbie Goodman.
    p.   cm. — (Prentice Hall's reality reading series)
  ISBN 0-13-174570-0
  1. Crime—United States—Case studies. 2. Criminal investigation—United States—Case studies. I.
Goodman, Debbie J. II. Title. III. Series.
  HV6789.G88 2007
  364.10973—dc22

                                                                    2006010687

Editor-in-Chief: Vernon R. Anthony
Executive Editor: Frank Mortimer, Jr.
Associate Editor: Sarah Holle
Marketing Manager: Adam Kloza
Editorial Assistant: Jillian Allison
Production Editor: Patty Donovan, Pine Tree Composition, Inc.
Production Liaison: Barbara Marttine Cappuccio
Director of Manufacturing and Production: Bruce Johnson
Managing Editor: Mary Carnis
Manufacturing Manager: Ilene Sanford
Manufacturing Buyer: Cathleen Petersen
Senior Design Coordinator: Mary Siener
Cover Designer: Brian Kane
Cover Image: Dorling Kindersley Media Library
Formatting and Interior Design: Pine Tree Composition, Inc.
Printing and Binding: R. R. Donnelley & Sons

Pearson Education LTD.
Pearson Education Singapore, Pte. Ltd
Pearson Education, Canada, Ltd
Pearson Education-Japan
Pearson Education Australia PTY, Limited
Pearson Education North Asia Ltd
Pearson Education de Mexico, S.A. de C.V.
Pearson Education Malaysia, Pte. Ltd

10 9 8 7 6 5 4 3 2 1
ISBN 0-13-174570-0
OCLC: 65407275

From Ron Grimming

To Karen, I thank you for your support, your understanding, and your love!

and

To the men and women who aspire to become members of the criminal justice profession, I encourage you to dream your dream, and then make it happen.

From Debbie J. Goodman

To Glenn and Connor, my heroes, I love you both more than words can express.

and

To the past, present, and future criminal justice professionals, thank you for your exemplary service to our communities.

Contents

Preface

Millions of viewers of modern television programming appear to have a fixation with reality-based shows that deal with street crime, the police, and the American judicial system. For many, there is a compelling interest to observe a day-in-the-life of one who protects and serves the public. For the first time ever, the leading publisher in the Criminal Justice industry, Prentice Hall, brings you, in written form: *The Criminal Justice Reality Reading Series: A Collection of True-Crime Cases.* In ten, easy-to-absorb handbooks, you will read about provocative, true cases that coincide with the most popular Criminal Justice courses offered at colleges, universities, and police academies throughout the United States. The handbooks are designed to enhance the theoretical textbook approach with the pragmatic and practical aspects of the field. The cases selected for this text coincide with *Part I Crimes:*

Crimes Against Persons	**Crimes Against Property**
Murder	Burglary
Forcible Rape	Arson
Robbery	Larceny-Theft
Aggravated Assault	Motor Vehicle Theft

Enjoy this first book in *The Reality Reading Series* which will provide you with the opportunity to study nationally recognized "True Crime Cases" and learn about the actual elements and definitions of Part I crimes. Additionally, you will become the investigator in each case, and as such you will reinforce your knowledge and understanding of Part I crimes by discussing elements of the offenses, investigative procedures, modus operandi, and the motivation for criminals to commit these crimes.

Because of the unique police-style manner in which the text has been written, it is recommended that this textbook be utilized in a supplemental capacity for a variety of academic and academy training classes to include:

- Introduction to Criminology
- Introduction to Criminal Justice
- Introduction to Policing/Law Enforcement Systems
- Criminal Law
- Constitutional Law
- Criminal Investigation

or

- As a stand-alone class focusing on special topics pertaining to case studies

An additional feature of this text is that it is designed to be utilized to promote group discussions and/or individualized assignments and research projects.

Enjoy this first book in *The Reality Reading Series* and the dialogue and discussion that will be generated during classroom interaction.

Best regards,
Ron Grimming
Debbie J. Goodman

Acknowledgments

The authors gratefully acknowledge the students, faculty, staff, and administrators at Miami Dade College in Miami, Florida, for their support.

A special thanks to the talented experts at Prentice Hall Publishing: Robin Baliszewski, Frank Mortimer, Adam Kloza, Sarah Holle, and the following reviewers: David Kotajarvi, Lakeshore Technical College; Kay Henriksen, MacMurray College; James Jengeleski, Shippensburg University; David Graff, Kent State University—Tuscaranas; and Jeff Magers, University of Louisville.

Thank you, Mary Greene, for your wonderful expertise involving manuscript coordination.

About the Authors

Ron Grimming

Ron Grimming has an extensive, and impressive, 33-year background in law enforcement. His career in law enforcement began in 1970 as a Special Agent with the Illinois State Police. He served in various investigative assignments including: special task forces targeting criminal activities associated with subversive groups, political and police corruption, illegal drugs, and financial crimes. He was promoted numerous times during his career, and attained the rank of Deputy Director of the Illinois State Police, supervising more than 2,500 officers assigned to the investigative and patrol divisions of the department.

In 1993 Grimming was appointed Director of the Florida Highway Patrol, where he managed the activities of 1,740 sworn officers and 528 civilian personnel. Grimming focused the patrol's mission on highway safety through traffic enforcement, accident investigation, prevention of highway violence, interdiction of illegal contraband, investigation of auto-theft, and the development of public safety education programs. Through Grimming's leadership, the Florida Highway Patrol received the recognition of being nationally accredited, after having its policies and operational procedures scrutinized by a panel of nationally recognized law enforcement experts. Also under Grimming's guidance, the patrol won the prestigious National Chief's Challenge, designating it as having the best traffic safety program in the nation.

During his law enforcement career, Grimming has served as General Chairman of the International Association of Chiefs of Police (IACP), State and Provincial Police Division, which represents the nation's state police and highway patrol organizations on the IACP Board of Directors. Grimming also served as Chairman of the IACP Organized Crime Committee, and President of the State Law Enforcement Chief's Association. Grimming has an extensive law enforcement training background having served on Florida's Criminal Justice Standards and Training Commission. He currently serves as Director of Miami-Dade College's School of Justice, which has responsibility for college criminal justice degree programs, as well as law enforcement, corrections, and security officer training for Miami-Dade County criminal justice agencies.

Debbie J. Goodman

Debbie J. Goodman, M.S., is the Chairperson of the School of Justice at Miami-Dade College. She holds a Master of Science degree in Criminal Justice from Florida International University and a Bachelor of Science degree in Criminology from Florida State University. Ms. Goodman specializes in a wide range of Criminal Justice topics, including: report writing, ethics, communications, human behavior, juvenile justice, criminology, criminal justice, and leadership. She is the author of three other Prentice Hall publications: *Report It In Writing, Enforcing Ethics,* and *Florida Crime and Justice.*

She is the originator and series editor of Prentice Hall's *PACTS: Police And Corrections Training Series.* Debbie J. Goodman is an adjunct faculty member in the College of Public Affairs at Florida International University and was honored in 2002 and 2005 by *Who's Who Among America's Teachers* as one of the nation's most talented college instructors. She is committed to providing quality education and training to police and corrections officers, as well as criminal justice students and practitioners. She resides in South Florida with her husband and son.

Introduction
Crime Reporting
in the United States

Before we evaluate eight stunning cases, we want to remind you of how crime is reported in the United States. In 1929, Congress mandated that the Federal Bureau of Investigation (FBI) implement the *Uniform Crime Report* (UCR). *UCR*, as it is known, tracks eight serious, or major, crimes, which include *homicide, forcible rape, robbery, aggravated assault, burglary, larceny-theft, motor vehicle theft*, and *arson*. These crimes are referred to as *Part I crimes* in the UCR system, and are incorporated into UCR reports each time an offense is reported to a law enforcement agency.

UCR also reports crime data on twenty-one other crime categories, which are known as *Part II crimes*. These include crimes such as *drug law violation, fraud, vandalism, gambling, prostitution, weapons crimes, disorderly conduct, driving under the influence, and similar types of less serious offenses.*

Part I crimes are divided into two basic categories: *crimes against persons (violent crimes) and crimes against property.*

The following chart lists the major Part I crimes by category:

Crimes Against Persons	Crimes Against Property
Murder	Burglary
Forcible Rape	Arson
Robbery	Larceny-Theft
Aggravated Assault	Motor Vehicle Theft

In reviewing and understanding UCR data, it is important to note that Part I crimes are counted in the system when these crimes are *reported* to police. Part II crimes, on the other hand, are counted and appear in UCR data based upon *arrests* of individuals.

As of 2003, law enforcement agencies active in the UCR program represented nearly 291 million U.S. inhabitants, which is approximately 93% of the country's total population. As these numbers point out, not all law enforcement agencies report their crime data to the UCR system, so the exact picture of crime in the United States is not 100% accurate. Also contributing to the vulnerability of the data is the *reliability* of information provided by each of the contributing law enforcement agencies. Historically, some police agencies have intentionally *under reported* crime to make their crime fighting efforts *appear* better than they actually are, while other agencies simply have invalid and inaccurate reporting processes. Also, it must be kept in mind that Part I crime data is based on offenses *reported* to police. For example, in the case of rape, it is estimated that only 1 in 4 rapes is reported. Nonetheless, UCR data, although not perfect, is an excellent overview of the crime problems in our nation, and a comparative tool to track crime increases and decreases over time.

Following a five year redesign, the UCR program is currently being converted to the more comprehensive and detailed *National Incident-Based Reporting System (NIBRS)*. NIBRS will provide detailed information about each criminal incident in 22 broad categories of offenses. Additional crimes have been added to the NIBRS system to provide a more modern and updated approach to crime reporting. Crimes such as pornography, identify theft, credit card fraud, and others will be reported in the new NIBRS system. Currently, about 4,300 law enforcement agencies contribute NIBRS data to the FBI annually. Although the NIBRS system was to have been in place some years ago, due to its reporting complexities, only 22 states are currently authorized to contribute NIBRS data. But, as of this writing, many more states are in the final stages of approval, and are expected to be approved contributors in the near future.

In addition to the FBI's UCR crime reporting process, the Bureau of Justice Statistics (BJS), another federal agency, collects crime statistics through its *National Crime Victimization*

Survey (NCVS). NCVS is intended to complement UCR so it collects data on the same major Part I crimes (except murder). However, NCVS defines some of the crimes differently. For example, UCR counts rape as only those offenses committed by a male against a female victim, whereas NCVS accounts for all rapes, to include female offenders and same-sex rapes. NCVS was also created to report those crimes not being reported to the police, to include information about victims and offenders. Data is collected through U.S. Census Bureau personnel surveying approximately 42,000 households and interviewing about 150,000 persons ages 12 and over.

At the present time, UCR crime information remains the primary source of data being utilized in the United States relative to crime collection and analysis. When the new NIBRS system becomes fully operational, UCR will eventually be phased out.

In the forthcoming chapters, you will have the opportunity to learn more about the UCR and study provocative, real crime cases in the UCR Part I crime series. Also, you will be placed in the role of the investigator at the conclusion of each chapter. In your investigative capacity, you will reinforce the learning process by responding to a series of questions, which will enable you to immediately apply your new knowledge in analyzing each case.

Criminal Justice

CHAPTER 1

Murder

DEFINITION

According to the FBI's Uniform Crime Report, murder is the unlawful killing of one human being by another.

Introduction

The term *murder* is a general term used to describe numerous offenses depending upon the jurisdiction. These include *first degree* and *second degree murder,* as well as *manslaughter, involuntary manslaughter, vehicular homicide,* and other similar crimes wherein one person unlawfully causes the death of another. These offenses vary from one state to another based upon the intent of the perpetrator when the crime was committed.

Murder, or *homicide* as it is often called, is considered by our society as the most serious and heinous of all criminal acts. Murders generally receive top billing by the news media, and homicides are given prime-time coverage on nightly television networks and front-page coverage in newspapers across the country. Because of their severity, homicides have become a reliable barometer of all violent crime. At the national level, no other crime is measured as accurately and precisely as murder, and no other crime is monitored more closely at a local, state, and national level. Because murder is such a serious crime, law

1

enforcement commits significant resources to handling these crimes. As a result, the offense of murder has the highest clearance rate of any of the "index crimes." In 2002, 64% of all homicides throughout the United States were solved.

The United States experienced 16,204 murders in 2002, but it should be noted that murder is the least statistically significant of the Part I crimes, with 5.6 homicides occurring for every 100,000 residents in the United States. This equates to one murder occurring every two minutes, nationally.

According to the Bureau of Justice Statistics (BJS), homicide rates nearly doubled from the mid 1960s to the late 1970s. Homicide rates peaked in 1980 at 10.2 per 100,000 population and declined to 8.0 per 100,000 in 1984. By the late 1980s and into the early 1990s, murder rates rose again and peaked in 1991 at 9.8 per 100,000 population. Since 1992 the murder rate has fallen dramatically to 5.6 murders per 100,000 population in 2002, and murders have remained stable, nationally, since then.

When considering homicide trends by gender, BJS 2002 data reflects that most victims and perpetrators of homicides are males as noted below:

- Male offender/male victim   65.1%
- Male offender/female victim   22.6%
- Female offender/male victim   9.9%
- Female offender/female victim   2.4%

Consequently, males were 3.4 times more likely than females to be murdered in 2002, but males were 10 times more likely than females to commit murder in 2002. BJS data also reflects that both male and female offenders are more likely to target male victims than female victims.

Among all homicide victims, women are particularly at risk for *intimate killings* (offender in relationship with victim), sex related homicides, and murders committed by arson or poison.

When considering other demographic characteristics, blacks are disproportionately represented as both homicide victims and perpetrators. In terms of rates per 100,000 population, data suggests blacks are 6 times more likely to be victimized and 7 times more likely to commit homicides than are whites.

When considering age as a factor, approximately one-third of murder victims, and almost half the offenders are under the age of 25. For both victims and offenders, the rate per 100,000 peaks in the 18–24-year-old age bracket. Although the number of homicides of children under age 5 increased over the past two decades, since 1997 rates have declined. In what is known as *infanticide* (murder of an infant under age 5), a parent is the perpetrator in the majority of instances as reflected below during the period 1976–2002:

- 31% were killed by fathers
- 30% were killed by mothers
- 23% were killed by male acquaintances
- 6% were killed by relatives
- 3% were killed by strangers

The other age category that is significant when considering homicide trends are senior citizens who are 65 years of age or older. About 5% of all homicides in the United States during 2002 were persons 65 years of age or older. Of this group, males 65 or older were slightly more likely than females to be homicide victims. Generally, older homicide victims are more likely to be killed during the commission of another crime than their younger counterparts.

When discussing the crime of murder it is essential that one understand the difference between what is referred to in many jurisdictions as *first degree* and *second degree murder. First degree murder is the premeditation and deliberate planning to unlawfully and intentionally kill another person. Second degree murder, on the other hand also requires the "malice aforethought" (intent) to unlawfully take the life of another, but is generally not planned by the perpetrator, and results from what is termed the "heat of passion."* First and second degree murder differ from manslaughter in many jurisdictions, in that *manslaughter is the killing of another person through gross negligence, but where the perpetrator did not intend the death of the victim, although his/her negligent actions caused the death.* An example of manslaughter would be a case in which two individuals got into a fight, one was punched by the other and fell to the ground, dying as a result of a skull fracture from his head hitting the pavement.

Law enforcement officials categorize murders in the following ways:

Spree Murders   Murders that occur at multiple locations with little time elapsed between the crimes. The Washington, DC sniper case is an example in which 10 people were shot and killed during a three-week period by John Muhammad and his 17-year-old accomplice.

Mass Murders   Murders that involve the killing of multiple victims, usually four or more, at one location, at one time. An example would be the Oklahoma City Federal Building bombing committed by Timothy McVeigh.

Serial Murders   Murders involving the killing of several victims over time in several different locations. These killings can occur over a period of months or even years, oftentimes with breaks occurring between the murders. An example of a serial murderer is the infamous BTK (Bind, Torture, Kill) killer, Dennis Rader, who admitted killing 10 women over nearly a 30 year period in the Wichita, Kansas area.

Murder: The Andrew Cunanan Case

Young, attractive, and smart, Andrew Cunanan possessed all of the necessary ingredients for success. With a 147 IQ, he was fluent in seven languages by the time he reached 21 years of age. His brilliant mind enabled him to interact with ease with groups of much older men. It was well known by Cunanan's circle of friends that he was gay. He never attempted to conceal his sexual persuasion, and easily dismissed those who didn't understand him.

Cunanan's childhood was mostly normal, except that his father, Modesto, who was Filipino, frequently argued with Andrew's mother, accusing her of being unfaithful. Modesto Cunanan bought expensive clothes for his son to wear to school, urged Andrew, the youngest of their children, to "be somebody, son." By age 12, Andrew's dress and demeanor at school became a point of contention with his classmates. Ultimately, Cunanan's parents transferred him to a private school in San Diego, where tuition was $7,000 per year. In his new school, Cunanan felt confused about his relationship and attraction toward males and females. He would compare the females to his mother, and none could come close to his mother whom he adored so much. Also, some of the girls frightened Cunanan, because they seemed too forward and assertive. Andrew had more interest in, and a greater attraction to, weaker children and most of those he was attracted to were males.

Based upon biographical information, Cunanan began his homosexual experience in his early teens, and seemed more satisfied and physically attracted to members of his own sex.

By his teens Cunanan had grown bigger than most of the male friends his age. His good looks, homosexual experiences, and engaging personality made it possible for him to frequent San Diego's gay bars where he would drink and socialize with older gay men.

After graduating from high school, Cunanan enrolled at the University of California, but his tendency to go from one gay bar to another affected his school work. As Cunanan immersed himself in the gay bar scene, it became obvious to him that the older, more mature, wealthy gay men, were willing to pay large sums of money to be in a relationship with a handsome, young gay man like Andrew.

Andrew Cunanan became a male prostitute, and was in high demand in San Diego's wealthy gay community. He was rewarded handsomely for his sexual services by these older men. One lover gave him an expensive car, and others took him to parties where he interacted with politicians and celebrities, and was provided large sums of cash and fancy clothing.

Cunanan eventually moved to San Francisco where he became a regular at the gay night clubs in the famous Castro section of town, which was well-known as the Las Vegas for gays. This was the life style with which Andrew Cunanan felt comfortable. He met a very wealthy gentleman there, a lawyer named Eli Gould. Through Gould, Andrew got access to Hollywood's elite super-models, and to the exclusive parties of the wealthy gay community.

One of the famous people Cunanan met at one of these parties was fashion icon Gianni Versace. Versace, who was gay, spotted Cunanan standing next to Eli Gould, and approached Cunanan saying, "I know you." They briefly talked and then Versace moved on.

Cunanan's gay relationships evolved into numerous sex orgies, where leather outfits, chains, and sexual whippings became pervasive. Andrew became a hot commodity in San Francisco's gay community. Cunanan underwent a change that would set the stage for the rest of his life. A darker side started to emerge, and the once friendly, outgoing Cunanan suddenly became mean spirited and angry. He said and did angry things, and this nasty attitude seemed to consume Cunanan's life. Once, when a friend visited Cunanan at his apartment, he noticed a number of pictures of Tom Cruise on display and made a comment about the picture. This caused Cunanan to go into a tirade cursing Nicole Kidman, Cruise's wife, saying that she "had" Cruise and he probably never would. According to Cunanan's friend, Cunanan spent a great deal of the evening violently complaining about Nicole Kidman.

As a result of his promiscuous life style, Cunanan developed AIDS symptoms, and although he went in for testing in early 1997, he never returned to get the test results. In addition to experiencing AIDS symptoms, Cunanan also had been deserted by his older, wealthy lovers, and he started to experience financial difficulties. Also contributing to Cunanan's downward psychological spiral was the belief that two of his young lovers, Jeff Trail and David Madson, were in a relationship. Cunanan became insanely jealous.

Jeff Trail moved to Minneapolis, Minnesota, where Cunanan visited him. While on one of his visits, Trail and Cunanan were at a restaurant when Cunanan spotted David Madson, a successful architect who had also moved to Minneapolis. Cunanan became very irritated when he saw Madson, and although he still was attracted to both men, he became more and more suspicious that they were having a relationship. In addition to his jealousy over what he suspected was Trail and Madson's relationship, he also envied both young men, who had become successful businessmen, something Cunanan never achieved.

The Murders Begin

After returning to California, his jealousy over Trail and Madson completely enveloped Cunanan, and in April of 1997, he phoned Trail in Minneapolis and accused him of having an affair with Madson. Although Trail denied it, the phone conversation became quite violent as Cunanan threatened to kill Trail. That evening, Cunanan purchased an airline ticket, flew to Minneapolis, and had David Madson pick him up at the airport. Cunanan went to Madson's apartment, located in an affluent area of Minneapolis. Madson offered to have Trail visit his house where both Madson and Trail tried to convince Cunanan that nothing was going on between them. Friends of Madson's from California had called him to warn him that Cunanan was dangerous and might do something stupid. Madson ignored the warning and believed that Cunanan was just going through a difficult time.

When Trail came to Madson's apartment the next night, an immediate tension developed between Cunanan and Trail. Despite Madson's efforts to calm the situation, an argument turned violent and physical between the two men. During the fight between Trail and Cunanan, Cunanan ran into the kitchen, found a hammer, and before either Trail or Madson could react, Cunanan hit Trail in the head multiple times. The viciousness of

Cunanan's blows to Trail's head resulted in blood splattering all over the room. Trail's lifeless body fell to the ground.

Madson was in shock at what he had witnessed, yet he found himself assisting Cunanan in putting Trail's body on a large rug and then rolling the rug around Trail's body. Trail's corpse was placed behind a couch for several days, while Cunanan and Madson decided what to do.

After Madson had not reported to work for several days, co-workers became concerned and contacted the building manager and asked him to check on Madson. When the manager entered the apartment, he found bloodstains on the walls and floor and then discovered Trail's body wrapped in a rug behind the couch.

When Cunanan and Madson realized that Trail's body had been discovered, they hurriedly left town in Madson's red Jeep Cherokee.

Meanwhile, back at Madson's apartment, police investigators found Andrew Cunanan's backpack, which contained identification that quickly included Cunanan as a suspect in the slaying of Jeff Trail. Additional evidence was obtained by police when they searched Trail's apartment and discovered a message on his phone recorder from Cunanan, inviting Trail to Madson's apartment.

Unfortunately for Madson, Cunanan's killing spree had just begun. Approximately forty-five miles from Minneapolis on a lonely country road, Cunanan pulled Madson's vehicle to a stop, pulled a .40 caliber handgun from his pocket, and shot his friend Madson three times, leaving his body on the side of the road.

Within a week of murdering Madson, Cunanan encountered his next victim: a 72-year-old, wealthy Chicago developer named Lee Miglin. While driving in an exclusive area north of the Chicago downtown area, Cunanan spotted Lee Miglin standing in front of his home. Miglin's wife was out of town on a business trip. Cunanan approached him on the sidewalk, and it is believed that he pulled a gun on Miglin and forced him into a garage next to the victim's townhouse. Cunanan tied Miglin's hands together and then put duct tape over Miglin's face, only leaving room for him to breathe.

Cunanan then brutally beat and kicked Miglin. He took a pair of pruning shears and stabbed Miglin in the chest several times. When Cunanan realized that Miglin was still breathing, he took a hacksaw and began cutting through Miglin's throat.

Still not finished, Cunanan placed Miglin's body under the wheels of Miglin's 1994 Lexus, and repeatedly drove the car over the body, smashing virtually every bone in Miglin's body.

Cunanan then casually entered Miglin's home where he fixed himself something to eat, watched a few videos, and then fell asleep in Miglin's bed. The next morning when Cunanan awoke, he stole several gold coins and then drove off in Miglin's green Lexus. Cunanan made no effort to conceal the fact that he was responsible for the murder of Miglin, having parked Madson's red Jeep Cherokee a block away with photographs of himself spread across the front seat in plain view.

The Investigation

In the wake of three murders in less than 10 days, spanning two states, the FBI entered the investigation. Andrew Cunanan was on the FBI's Top Ten Most Wanted List. Newspapers and television stations showed photographs of Cunanan. Authorities were desperate to catch Cunanan before he killed again.

While driving east toward Philadelphia, Cunanan used the Lexus's car phone, which police were monitoring. Authorities put out "all points bulletins" to be on the look-out for Cunanan and the green Lexus. Cunanan heard the news stories on the car's radio and realized that he had blundered by using the cell phone. Cunanan threw the phone out of the car window, and began looking for a safe place to hide. Cunanan realized he had to get rid of the Lexus or it would only be a matter of time until police caught him. Cunanan found the perfect hiding place—a cemetery in Pennsville, New Jersey.

As Cunanan drove through the cemetery, he noticed a red truck parked in front of the caretaker's house. Cunanan pulled over and approached the door and knocked. The occupant, William Reese, came to the door, and within seconds, Cunanan had pulled the .40 caliber gun and shot Reese. Cunanan located the keys to Reese's red Chevy pick-up truck and fled New Jersey, heading south.

As the police continued with their investigation, wanted posters were disseminated nationally with the many different looks that Andrew Cunanan used in changing his appearance, as he went from one location to another.

As Cunanan's reign of terror spread across the country, the public, police, and Cunanan's friends and family speculated as to what caused Andrew Cunanan to murder. In San Francisco's gay community, many believed that it was either jealousy, or the fact that Cunanan believed he had AIDS, that caused the monster within Cunanan to surface. With four people dead, when and where would Cunanan strike next?

Authorities were not sure who Cunanan's next victim would be. Andrew chose his next destination, glamorous Miami Beach, where his next victim was known to have a residence. Cunanan made little effort to hide out, frequenting gay night clubs, and mingling with crowds of people on Collins Avenue for nearly two months. When Cunanan arrived in Miami Beach on May 10, 1997, he parked the stolen red truck he took from Reese in a public parking garage near the Hotel Normandy where he stayed. Cunanan continued to think about his next victim. He became bolder as he was comforted by the fact that the FBI and police were unable to find him.

Versace—The Famous Victim

During the afternoons, Cunanan walked to 11th Street in South Beach where Gianni Versace's mansion was located, just across the street from the ocean, in hopes of seeing the man who would be his next victim.

Versace, a successful fashion designer with profits in excess of $900 million dollars per year, had returned from a lengthy business trip to Europe. He told a friend he was looking forward to some down time and privacy at his home on Miami Beach. Versace usually relaxed at Miami Beach's gay bars in the evenings, and walked to the News Cafe for his favorite coffee in the morning.

Unaware he was being stalked, Versace was followed by Cunanan when he departed from the News Cafe on July 15, 1997, and began walking home. Why Cunanan wanted to kill Versace is subject to much speculation, but FBI files indicate that Versace had refused to give Cunanan a modeling job, which may have angered Cunanan. As Versace approached his mansion, he was totally unaware that Cunanan had been following him for blocks. When Versace took the key from his pocket to open the iron gate that surrounded the mansion, Andrew Cunanan moved in behind Versace, and at point-blank range, fired two .40 caliber bullets into Versace's head. After killing Versace, Cunanan calmly walked away from the scene.

After the Versace murder, a media frenzy developed and every investigative step undertaken by the FBI and local police was monitored and reported on daily. Hundreds of additional FBI agents and local police officers were summoned to participate in the Versace investigation. Investigators operating under the microscope of the national media were ridiculed for several perceived blunders.

Authorities had confirmed sightings of Cunanan in Miami Beach prior to the Versace murder, but, according to the media, never told citizens, who, particularly in the gay community, were outraged that the killer had been moving freely among them. In fact, four days before Versace was killed, Cunanan was spotted in a sandwich shop, but by the time police arrived, he had disappeared.

The other perceived mistake by investigators was the fact that William Reese's red pick-up truck was left abandoned in a public parking garage for more than two months and was not discovered until after Versace's death. Many queried authorities as to why every parking garage and street had not been checked for Cunanan's vehicle, since authorities had information that he was in Miami Beach.

But the biggest oversight by authorities occurred on July 7, eight days before Versace was killed. Cunanan was struggling for money and went into a local pawn shop to sell one of the gold coins that he had taken from Lee Miglin's house in Chicago. Procedures in the pawn shop required Cunanan to produce two forms of identification and to sign a receipt. Cunanan produced two forms of identification, signed his real name, and listed his address as the Normandy Plaza Hotel. The pawn shop was required by law to fax the information to the Miami Beach Police Department. The faxed form went unnoticed at the police department until hours after Versace's death, because the clerk who received the forms was on vacation.

Law enforcement problems continued, although police were aware that Cunanan might be staying at the Normandy Hotel. When SWAT team members arrived, the hotel accidentally directed police to the wrong hotel room. When police entered the room, they found it empty. Two days later, the hotel recognized its mistake and called police with the correct room number. By now, Cunanan had left the Normandy Hotel, but he had left a few personal items behind.

On July 23, 1997, eight days after Gianni Versace was murdered in front of his mansion, police got the break for which they had been waiting. A caretaker who was checking a houseboat, moored in the Indian Creek canal, that belonged to his boss, a German millionaire, noticed the door to the houseboat was ajar. Upon entering the residence, the caretaker looked around and found nothing out of place. Then, he went upstairs to the bedroom area where he was met by a startled young man, who suddenly closed the door to the bedroom. The caretaker immediately thought that the man must be the fugitive that the police were looking for. Once he got outside, he called the police to report his encounter.

In a matter of minutes, the houseboat was surrounded on all sides including police boats in the water, SWAT teams on the ground, and helicopters in the air. After more than a three hour stand-off, police decided to move in when Andrew Cunanan refused to respond to calls from the bull-horn. At approximately 8:15 p.m., officers entered and searched the downstairs area of the houseboat, before moving upstairs. Authorities carefully went from room to room, and suddenly spotted Andrew Cunanan's lifeless body next to the bed, dead of a single, self-inflicted gunshot to the head.

Perhaps the story of Andrew Cunanan is best summarized by Vernon Geberth, author of *Practical Homicide Investigation*, who wrote of Cunanan, "If you take a look at the dynamics of the killing of (Versace), he was basically killing the person that he could never be . . . a lot of folks do this to feel a sense of superiority over the police."

You're the Investigator

1. Analyze the impact of age, race, and gender on homicide rates in the United States.

   _____

   _____

   _____

   _____

   _____

   _____

   _____

   _____

   _____

   _____

   _____

2. Distinguish between the elements of murder in the first degree and manslaughter.

   _____

   _____

   _____

   _____

   _____

   _____

   _____

   _____

   _____

   _____

   _____

3. Identify and discuss the three categories of multiple murders.

_____

_____

_____

_____

_____

_____

_____

_____

_____

_____

4. Analyze and discuss the motive for Cunanan's murders of Jeff Trail and David Madson.

_____

_____

_____

_____

_____

_____

_____

_____

_____

5. Describe the evidence authorities seized to identify Cunanan as a suspect in Trail's murder. Discuss the legal implications regarding the admissibility of the evidence.

_____

_____

_____

_____

_____

_____

_____

_____

_____

_____

_____

6. Identify and analyze the evidentiary items of evidence linking Cunanan to Lee Miglin's murder.

_____

_____

_____

_____

_____

_____

_____

_____

_____

_____

7. Identify and discuss investigative strategies and techniques
   that investigators used to track Cunanan after he fled
   Chicago.

_____

_____

_____

_____

_____

_____

_____

_____

_____

_____

8. Discuss the investigative theories authorities developed pertaining to Cunanan's rationale for murdering Gianni Versace.

_____

_____

_____

_____

_____

_____

_____

_____

_____

_____

9. Discuss the opportunities that law enforcement had to capture Cunanan before the Versace murder.

_____

_____

_____

_____

_____

_____

_____

_____

_____

_____

10. Describe the various theories regarding why Cunanan murdered his five victims (i.e., psychological, sociological, economic).

_____

_____

_____

_____

_____

_____

_____

_____

_____

_____

_____

CHAPTER 2

Forcible Rape

DEFINITION

According to the FBI's Uniform Crime Report, rape is defined as unlawful sexual intercourse achieved through force and without consent.

Introduction

As students and practitioners of Criminal Justice, you know that one of the most serious and traumatic personal crimes one can endure is that of rape.

In broad terms, the word *rape* has been applied to a variety of sexual attacks and may include same-sex rape and the rape of a male by a female.

For purposes of our discussion and an overview of a startling case to come, there are additional categories of this particular crime of which we need to be mindful.

"Forcible rape is defined by the Uniform Crime Report (UCR) as the carnal knowledge of a female forcibly and against her will." The FBI defines forcible rape as *"Unlawful sexual intercourse with a female, by force and against her will, and without consent."*

In today's society, there are other specific categories of rape that have evolved which are also worth mentioning.

Date Rape is the unlawful, forceful sexual intercourse with a female against her will that occurs within the scope of a dating relationship.

Typically, these crimes often occur in environments (high school, college, parties, etc.) where individuals are acquainted, which is why *date rape* is often referred to as *acquaintance rape.*

Recent data on the topic suggests that *date rape drugs* play a role in the commission of this crime. Law enforcement officials cite *Rohypnol* or *"Ruffies"* as a popular drug of choice among perpetrators of date rape, as it is tasteless, can easily be dissolved into one's drink, and leaves one unconscious for hours. The drug makes its victim particularly vulnerable to a sexual assault because one literally has the feeling of being "out of it" for an extended period of time.

Marital Rape has found its place in statutes to mean a sexual assault that takes place between a husband and wife, without consent.

Statutory Rape is defined as *the unlawful sexual intercourse that occurs with a minor.* A *minor* is one who has not yet reached the age of maturity or adult status. This varies by state.

As criminologists, we know that rape is a crime that is highly reported (approximately 150,000 rapes were reported throughout the United States in 2004.) This equates to a forcible rape occurring every five minutes, nationally. It is also a crime with a high clearance rate (solved by police). The question many have is, "Why?" Why do people rape? As we know, the answers vary:

- Dominance
- Power
- Humiliation
- Violation
- Lust

One of the most startling rape cases involving all of the factors identified above (dominance, power, humiliation, violation, and lust) is the case of Paul Bernardo and Karla Homolka.

Sex, Lies, Rape, and Murder:
The Paul Bernardo/Karla Homolka Case

In the 1990s, two attractive young people, Paul and Karla, started dating, fell in love, got engaged, then married, much the way thousands of couples do each year. The difference between this couple and others is that Paul and Karla were involved in a vicious rape and killing spree that would continue for years until they were caught and sentenced.

Paul was a handsome, professional accountant. Karla was a pretty veterinary employee. They loved each other and would do anything for one another. (Even kidnap, rape, and murder!)

One day, Paul was upset that Karla was not a virgin when they met. He wanted to figure out a way for her to "right the wrong." He decided that she could make it up to him by having her arrange for Paul to have sex with Karla's younger sister, Tammy Homolka. One night in December at a holiday party, Paul gave Tammy drinks (laced with halcyon, a sedative). Soon, Tammy lay unconscious on the couch, where Paul raped her and videotaped the crime. Karla stood by as Tammy choked to death on her vomit. That was Rape #1.

With Tammy dead, Paul soon convinced Karla to find him a "replacement virgin." Wanting Paul to be happy, Karla found the perfect virgin, Jane, a neighborhood teenager who even looked like Karla's dead sister, Tammy.

After providing Jane with alcoholic drinks (again laced with halcyon), Karla proceeded to have sex with Jane first, as Paul videotaped. Then, Paul raped Jane, as well as engaged in brutal, oral sex with her. Jane lived through the ordeal, remembering nothing of the crime perpetrated against her as she was completely "knocked out" from the drinks and drugs.

Paul's depravity continued when, in 1991, a teenager named Leslie Mahaffy met Paul Bernardo at 2:00 a.m. one morning when she was locked out of her parents' house. This time his approach (modus operandi) was different from the two previous crimes. This time Karla wasn't around and he was totally in control. Paul pulled a knife on Leslie, forced her into his car, and brought the 14-year-old home. Karla was asleep in the house and woke up to find Leslie naked and blindfolded. Paul demanded Karla to have sex with Leslie as he videotaped the scene. After Karla finished with the teenager, Paul moved in for the "rough stuff" while Karla held the camera. Leslie screamed in pain but her cry for help would not be heard. Leslie's partially dismembered body was discovered by boaters in Lake Gibson, tied to five concrete blocks, about 2 weeks after her abduction by Paul Bernardo.

The next crime took place on April 16, 1992, and involved the abduction of 14-year-old Kristen French. Paul and Karla abducted her outside of a church parking lot. Again, the ordeal endured by this young girl was different from the preceding crimes. This time over the course of 1–2 days (captured on videotape), Paul repeatedly defecated on Kristin, urinated on her, viciously and brutally raped her, and then killed her. The killing was not videotaped. On April 30, 1992, Kristen French's nude body was found in a ditch. Because Kristen's body was not dismembered like Leslie Mahaffy's, investigators concluded that the rapes and murders of the two teenagers were not related.

The Investigation

Canadian police officials focused their investigation in the Niagara Falls area because Holmolka and Bernardo had abducted young women in the St. Catharine area of Canada. After the bodies of Leslie Mahaffy and Kristen French were found, the Ontario government established the Green Ribbon Task Force to investigate the murders and rapes of these young women.

During their investigation, Paul Bernardo's name surfaced as a result of tips that were provided to the police by friends of Bernardo. Although several detectives stopped by Bernardo's residence to interview him, no solid evidence existed to implicate him. However, two of the detectives assigned to the Green Ribbon Task Force discovered that Bernardo had been a suspect in several rapes in the Scarborough area and that blood and saliva samples had been taken from him, but were never analyzed by the laboratory. Because of pressure from investigators, the lab in Toronto finally conducted the forensic analysis on Bernardo's blood, which confirmed, through semen comparison taken from the victims, that Bernardo had, in fact, raped the three women in Scarborough.

Unfortunately, due to the laboratory delay, Bernardo remained free to rape and murder several more young women.

Once detectives received the news from the laboratory, they immediately put Bernardo under surveillance, and in so doing, learned that he had been charged with assaulting his wife, Karla, whom he had punched in the face several times, and blackened both of her eyes.

Investigators seized the opportunity to interview Karla Homolka, who was in hiding from her husband. She feared he would beat her again. During the interviews, Karla realized that investigators had linked the Scarborough rapes with the murders of Mahaffy and French in St. Catharine. Karla Homolka secured an attorney and, through a deal with prosecutors, agreed to testify against her husband in the murders/rapes of Mahaffy and French.

Finally, in 1993, Paul Bernardo was arrested and his trial began in 1995, where he was convicted on all charges against him, including murder, rape, and kidnapping. Karla was sentenced to 12 years in prison in exchange for cooperating and testifying against Paul. Under Canadian law, Bernardo can apply for parole after serving 25 years in prison, although based upon the nature of his crimes, it is highly unlikely he would ever be paroled.

You're the Investigator

1. Identify and describe the rationales for Paul Bernardo and
   Karla Homolka perpetrating such violent acts.

   _____

   _____

   _____

   _____

   _____

   _____

   _____

   _____

   _____

   _____

   _____

2. Discuss the reasons you believe Karla agreed to participate
   in sex and violence at Paul's request.

   _____

   _____

   _____

   _____

   _____

   _____

   _____

   _____

   _____

   _____

_____

_____

3. Analyze the motivation for Paul and Karla videotaping their crimes.

_____

_____

_____

_____

_____

_____

_____

_____

_____

_____

_____

4. Compare and contrast the legal issues associated with Karla testifying against her husband in exchange for a 12-year sentence.

_____

_____

_____

_____

_____

_____

_____

_____

_____

_____

_____

_____

5. What is a just punishment for someone who engages in kidnapping, rape, and murder?

_____

_____

_____

_____

_____

_____

_____

_____

_____

_____

6. As the investigator, if you could question Paul today, what would you ask him?

_____

_____

_____

_____

_____

_____

_____

_____

_____

_____

_____

_____

7. As the investigator, if you could question Karla today, what would you ask her?

_____

_____

_____

_____

_____

_____

_____

_____

_____

_____

8. Identify and discuss the reasons you believe (or not) that Paul and Karla could successfully utilize the insanity defense.

_____

_____

_____

_____

_____

_____

_____

_____

_____

_____

_____

9. Describe why you think Paul became more violent with each attack.

_____

_____

_____

_____

_____

_____

_____

_____

_____

_____

10. Describe why you think Paul enjoyed degrading and humiliating young females.

_____

_____

_____

_____

_____

_____

_____

_____

_____

_____

CHAPTER 3

Robbery

DEFINITION

According to the FBI's Uniform Crime Report, robbery is defined as taking, or attempting to take, anything of value from the care, custody, or control of a person or persons by force or by the threat of force or violence, with the intent to permanently or temporarily deprive.

Some jurisdictions refer to a *robbery committed with a firearm or other deadly weapon as Armed Robbery. Armed Robbery* in most jurisdictions is considered a more significant offense because of the potential for injury to the victim. It is generally punishable with a more severe sentence. As an example, many jurisdiction statutes categorize robbery with a weapon (armed robbery), a non-probationable offense, requiring a mandatory jail sentence for the perpetrator upon conviction.

Introduction

Robbery is generally regarded as one of the most heinous crimes committed in our society. Due to its violent nature, it is widely reported in the media, and our prison population has a large segment of its inmates imprisoned for long periods of time as a result of robbery convictions.

Robbery, which is sometimes confused with other crimes such as theft and burglary, *is a crime against the person in which the offense occurs when the perpetrator confronts the victim, and through the threatened or actual use of force or violence, takes property or money from the victim.*

In 2003, the United States had an estimated 413,402 robbery offenses, which was nearly a 2% decrease from 2002. This equates to one robbery every 1.2 minutes, nationally.

The rate, which was estimated at 142 robberies per 100,000 population, decreased nearly 3% from 2002. The Uniform Crime Report (UCR) estimated that nearly 30% of all violent crime in the United States during 2003 was due to robbery offenses.

During the course of these robberies, victims collectively lost an estimated $514 million dollars in 2003, which equates to an average dollar loss of nearly $1,244 dollars per robbery offense.

Because of the nature of a robbery offense, wherein the taking or attempted taking of property occurs in the presence of the victim, robbery crimes are extremely dangerous due to the face-to-face confrontation between the perpetrator and the victim. In 2003, offenders used firearms in 41.8% of robberies, strong arm tactics (hands, fists, feet, etc.) in 39.9% of robberies, and edge weapons (knives) in 8.9% of robberies. According to the Bureau of Justice Statistics, firearms are discharged in 20% of all robberies, which obviously creates the potential for great harm to the victim or an innocent bystander.

It is also important to note in the case of robbery crimes, that they often occur in conjunction with other crimes, such as murder, rape, and burglary. In many instances, the murder of the victim may have occurred during the course of an armed robbery, either because the victim resisted or because the perpetrator became more violent. Likewise, what may start as a burglary may turn into a robbery, because the perpetrator is confronted by the victim, and the perpetrator reacts in a violent way toward the victim, oftentimes inflicting serious injury.

Robbery can also be a difficult crime for law enforcement agencies to solve. According to the Bureau of Justice Statistics, law enforcement agencies cleared only 26% of robbery cases in 2003. This low solution rate can be attributed to a number of factors, including the defendant(s) concealing one's identity to avoid identification, and witnesses who were frightened due to the use of force, and could not provide detailed descriptions to assist the police in identifying and locating the robbery suspect(s).

The Great Lufthansa Airline Robbery

Lufthansa Airlines employee, Louis Werner, was the classic example of a compulsive and decadent gambler, who bet on long shots to generate enough income to support his estranged wife, girlfriend, three children, and loan shark, on a $15,000 annual salary. By 1978, Werner's gambling activities had him in debt to bookies for more than $18,000. Pressed to pay back the money he owed, Werner began looking for an easy way out of his dilemma. He thought it would be a good idea to steal from his employer.

This was the second time Werner planned to rob his employer. In October 1976, Werner had stolen more than $22,000 in foreign currency from one of Lufthansa's cargo buildings. The next day, Werner took the money in a cardboard box to his co-worker, Peter Gruenwald's house on Long Island for safekeeping. During the next several days, Werner and Gruenwald were able to take the foreign currency to foreign exchange banks, and convert it to U.S. currency.

Less than two years later, with pressure mounting from the bookies to whom Werner owed money, he felt compelled to make an even bigger score to settle his gambling debt. By August of 1978, Werner and Gruenwald had joined forces to rob their employer again. Werner and Gruenwald provided detailed descriptions of the Lufthansa facility, and the exact time that large sums of currency were stored at the cargo facility to a group of men that would actually perform the robbery.

To find the team of robbers to conduct the robbery, Werner contacted his bookie, Frank Menna, who in turn contacted Martin Krugman, another bookie with whom Menna ultimately placed bets. Krugman had permitted Menna to let Werner get into debt knowing that at one point Werner would become desperate and provide information on a robbery opportunity. Krugman contacted a man named Henry Hill, who worked for a very violent organized crime figure by the name of James Burke. Burke, whose crew of thieves hung out at a place called Robert's Lounge, sent one of his crew members, Joseph Manri, to meet with Werner, and got details of the robbery plan. Manri was the only member of the robbery team Werner met, protecting Burke and the other members if something went wrong.

The Robbery

Burke gathered a group of experienced thieves to carry out the robbery, including Angelo Sepe, Tommy DeSimone, Louis Cafora, Joe Manri, and Frenchy McMahon. In addition, Burke's son Frank drove one of the vehicles, and Edwards, another crew member, would dispose of the getaway van after the heist. Each of the gang members received $10,000–$50,000, depending upon which aspect of the robbery they participated. This amount was based upon a percentage of the estimated $2 million take. Werner, on the other hand, received a flat 10% of the total taken during the heist.

Burke's gang became discouraged waiting for Werner to call and notify them that a large amount of money was being stored at Lufthansa's cargo terminal, but finally, on the afternoon of December 8, 1978, the call from Werner finally came. After making final arrangements over the weekend, the robbers planned to hit the terminal Monday morning, December 11, at about 3:00 a.m.

It was terribly cold that morning, as the van with gang members inside pulled up to the front of the cargo terminal. Four of the six gang members in the van exited, and went into the terminal building. As the gang was advised by Werner, the security guard was on a scheduled break, which permitted the gang to easily enter the facility. At gunpoint, they began capturing employees. A total of six employees were immediately herded into a lunch room, where they were handcuffed and forced to lie face down on the floor.

Meanwhile, the two gang members who were waiting in the van got edgy. As they waited in the van, they became increasingly nervous and began sweating because the plan was behind schedule. Eventually they took their masks off to cool down. Just as they did, the two were frightened by the appearance of a Lufthansa delivery van driver, who pulled up next to them. The driver, Kerry Whalen, thought nothing of the other van, assuming that it also was making a delivery. As Whalen proceeded into the building, he was confronted by one of the armed robbers, and was told to get into the van. Whalen refused and started to run when he was tackled by the robber, and struck several times in the head with the robber's gun. The bleeding Whalen was returned to the van, and forced to lie down on the floor of the vehicle.

In the meantime, the security officer heard the commotion involving Whalen, and went to check it out. As the officer investigated the noise, he was confronted by another gunman, who still had his mask off. The officer noted the distinct features of the robber, before being ordered to lie down beside Whalen on the floor of the van.

Ultimately, Whalen and the security officer were forced to walk to the lunch room, where they were ordered to lie face down on the floor with the other employees. With all the employees now either tied or handcuffed, the gunmen turned their attention to Rudi Eirich, the night manager, and ordered him to open the vault. It was obvious to Eirich that the robbers were aware of the alarm system, and they told Eirich that men were at his home, and would kill his family if he did not do as instructed. Eirich followed the robber's instructions, and in minutes, the vault was opened revealing what the gang was after.

The robbers took a total of 72 cartons full of untraceable money, and placed it in the getaway vehicle. After taking car keys from the pockets of their captives, the robbers fled the Lufthansa cargo terminal after being there for nearly an hour and twenty minutes. The robbers sped away in the van and back-up vehicle, and exited the airport undetected.

The robbers drove to Brooklyn, NY, and went to an auto repair business where Jimmy Burke was waiting for them. The boxes of cash were taken from the getaway van, and placed in two other vehicles. Jimmy Burke and his son Frank left in one car, and four of the other robbers drove off in the second vehicle. Edwards, the remaining robber, stayed behind to dispose of the van.

The Largest Robbery Ever

At the time of the Lufthansa robbery, the FBI indicated it was the largest cash robbery in the history of the United States, with more than $5 million in cash, and $850,000 in jewelry taken.

The magnitude of the robbery immediately resulted in four law enforcement agencies' resources being focused on solving the crime. In addition to the New York Port Authority Police,

Queens District Attorney's Detective Squad, and the New York City Police Department, the FBI assigned dozens of its agents in an attempt to solve the case.

The police agencies immediately came to the determination that the robbery was an inside job, and each agency began soliciting information from its core of informants in an attempt to get leads in the case. The efforts of the police agencies proved helpful, as the names of Tommy DeSimone, Angelo Sepe, and Frank Burke surfaced as suspects in the heist.

Additionally, a couple of witnesses at the scene of the robbery had seen two of the robbers with their masks off. They provided excellent descriptions to the police who were able to develop sketches of two of the suspects. These witnesses were also able to provide a good description of the white Ford Econoline van used by the robbers.

Unfortunately, a negative turn of events occurred when law enforcement agencies learned that the money's serial numbers would be untraceable, because the cash shipped from Europe to the United States was from dollars exchanged abroad by military personnel, American tourists, and U.S. business executives. To the disbelief of law enforcement, and the delight of the robbers, the money would be impossible to identify and trace.

In an interesting turn of events, the robber Edwards, who was supposed to have taken the van to a car shredder, instead decided to park it on a Brooklyn street. Police discovered the van which had been reported stolen earlier by a couple from Long Island. During the crime scene processing of the van, several fingerprints were retrieved from inside the van, and several pieces of evidence were left in the van.

A day after the van was found, the robbery crew was having a Christmas party at Robert's Lounge. Much of the discussion centered around the van's discovery, and the fact that Edwards had not followed instructions to have the car shredded. Even though the van discussion was the predominant theme, Edwards was present at the party and began to make disparaging comments about how other robbery crew members were given some share of the proceeds, and he had not received any. Edwards even openly remarked about how the Mafia guys got all those millions from the airport.

Because of his stupidity in not destroying the van, and his comments at the party about the heist, Edwards became the first casualty of the robbery. On December 18, Edwards was shot six times in the back of the head by one of the gang members at the request of one of the organized crime families, to punish Edwards and prevent him from talking to anyone else about the robbery.

The Investigation

Although law enforcement was not successful in finding the money from the Lufthansa heist, they pursued those they believed were responsible for the daring robbery. According to the Assistant United States Attorney handling the case, "There was never any mystery about who robbed Lufthansa." Burke, Sepe, and DeSimone were the focus of law enforcement's investigation within a matter of hours after the robbery. A Colombo organized crime family member, who was an informant for the FBI, told his agent handler that Burke was the organizer of the robbery. Also, the police were assisted by two of the robbery victims, who identified two of the robbers as Angelo Sepe and Tommy DeSimone.

The initial arrest in the case came on February 17, 1979, when the FBI arrested Angelo Sepe. Sepe subsequently was released when it was discovered that search warrants executed at Sepe's home were not served properly. Although guns and drugs were discovered in the residence, no evidence of the Lufthansa robbery was discovered.

On March 23, 1979, the charges relating the Lufthansa robbery were dropped against Sepe. However, Sepe violated probation for associating with another known felon, James Burke. Eventually, Burke was arrested for violating his probation for associating with Sepe, a known felon.

Although prosecutors had several of the principals responsible for the Lufthansa robbery in jail on other charges, no one had been charged with the actual robbery. Authorities turned their focus on Peter Gruenwald and Louis Werner, the Lufthansa employees who were suspected of providing inside information.

Gruenwald was initially subpoenaed to appear before a federal grand jury investigating the robbery. When authorities learned that Gruenwald was planning a trip out of the country, the FBI immediately arrested Gruenwald as a material witness, and placed him in jail. After being held overnight, investigators questioned Gruenwald, and he finally agreed to cooperate concerning his and Werner's role in the 1976 and 1978 Lufthansa robberies. With information provided by Gruenwald, FBI agents arrested Menna, who was one of Werner's bookies. Menna immediately requested immunity, and agreed to testify against Werner.

Law enforcement wanted several additional key pieces of evidence before arresting Werner. Agents learned that Werner bragged to both his wife and girlfriend about his role in the robbery. Both women were questioned by police, and both admitted that Werner confirmed his role in the robbery to them. Although Werner's wife's statement could not be used against Werner due to the privileged nature of their conversation, Werner's girlfriend's testimony was provided to the grand jury.

On February 20, 1979, Werner was arrested for his role in the robbery, and on February 23, bond was set at $1 million.

Although authorities attempted to get Werner to testify against his accomplices, Werner consistently refused to cooperate. Finally, on May 16, 1979, Werner was found guilty of three of the six charges filed against him, including the planning and carrying out of the 1976 Lufthansa theft of $22,000, as well as the 1978 $5.8 million Lufthansa robbery.

Immediately before Werner's trial, and after his conviction, several crew members from Burke's gang, and associates of theirs, were found mysteriously shot to death. In some instances, bodies were found in cars and in others, bodies were washed ashore after having been killed. The dead included Joseph Manri, Parnell Edwards, Robert McMahon, and Paolo LiCristi.

On June 29, Werner was sentenced to 15 years in prison, and fined $25,000 for his role in the Lufthansa robbery. Although prosecutors had finally succeeded in convicting Werner of the Lufthansa robbery, they continued to be frustrated in their efforts to charge the robbery's mastermind, James Burke.

Finally, the break the authorities were looking for happened. During the debriefing of another informant, who was associated with one of the gang members, information was provided that linked Burke to fixing a basketball game in Boston. It was just the break authorities needed. Federal prosecutors subsequently indicted Burke, and four other defendants, including a former

Boston College player. On November 23, 1981, all five defendants were convicted of racketeering and sports bribery. Burke was given a 20 year sentence in federal prison.

James Burke's conviction on the Boston College sports fixing charges was a "bitter sweet" victory for prosecutors, since they still had not been able to gather enough evidence to charge Burke with the Lufthansa robbery. The government continued to pursue Burke, even though he was confined to a federal prison. Eventually, through information provided by Henry Hill, another gang member, Burke, in 1985, was convicted of killing Richard Eaton over a $250,000 cocaine deal. As a result of Burke's conviction on the murder charge, he was sentenced to life in prison.

In July of 1984, another major player in the robbery was found dead in his basement. Authorities would later learn that Angelo Sepe was killed by Mafia hit men, as a result of a robbery he had committed on a mob-connected drug dealer.

The only remaining crew member in the Lufthansa robbery crew, James Burke's son, Frank Burke, was found shot to death in Brooklyn, NY, on May 18, 1987. A 46-year-old drug dealer was arrested several days later for young Burke's murder.

The final chapter in one of America's most complex and bizarre robberies occurred when James Burke died in 1996 of cancer while serving a life sentence in state prison. Interestingly, Louis Werner was the only person ever to be convicted of the Lufthansa robbery, and to date, no arrests have been made for the murders associated with the robbery. Today, more than 25 years after the robbery, the bodies of several of the gang members who were reported missing after the robbery remain missing, along with nearly $5.8 million dollars, from what, at the time, was the largest robbery in U.S. history.

You're the Investigator

1. Identify and describe the elements of the crime of robbery.

   _____

   _____

   _____

   _____

   _____

   _____

   _____

   _____

   _____

   _____

2. Compare and contrast the crimes of robbery and armed robbery. Why is armed robbery considered a more serious crime?

   _____

   _____

   _____

   _____

   _____

   _____

   _____

   _____

   _____

   _____

3. Why did the investigating agencies come to the conclusion that the Lufthansa robbery was an inside job, and what important investigative resource provided names of suspects to the authorities?

_____

_____

_____

_____

_____

_____

_____

_____

_____

_____

_____

_____

4. Identify and discuss the investigative problems that prevented authorities from tracing the cash stolen from Lufthansa Airlines.

_____

_____

_____

_____

_____

_____

_____

_____

_____

_____

5. Identify and analyze the significant piece of evidence police discovered left abandoned by the robbers. What critical physical evidence was discovered?

_____

_____

_____

_____

_____

_____

_____

_____

_____

_____

_____

6. Authorities had insufficient evidence to arrest Jimmy Burke and Angelo Sepe for the Lufthansa robbery. Describe the circumstances under which the authorities were able to arrest both subjects.

_____

_____

_____

_____

_____

_____

_____

_____

_____

_____

_____

7. Identify the only individual who was convicted of the Lufthansa robbery, explain why he was the only one convicted, and describe the evidence used to convict him.

_____

_____

_____

_____

_____

_____

_____

_____

_____

_____

_____

8. List and discuss five reasons why individuals commit robbery.

_____

_____

_____

_____

_____

_____

_____

_____

_____

_____

_____

_____

9. Discuss why you believe (or not) that the value of money or property taken in a robbery should affect the sentence imposed.

_____

_____

_____

_____

_____

_____

_____

_____

_____

_____

_____

10. Discuss effective crime prevention strategies for preventing robberies.

_____

_____

_____

_____

_____

_____

_____

_____

_____

_____

_____

CHAPTER 4

Aggravated Assault

DEFINITION

*According to the FBI's Uniform Crime Report,
aggravated assault is defined as: an unlawful attack
by one person upon another for the purpose of
inflicting severe or aggravated bodily injury.*

In many jurisdictions throughout the United States, however, what is defined in the UCR as aggravated assault may actually be categorized as several different types of crime. For purposes of clarification, the following examples are provided to assist you in distinguishing among these offenses.

Simple Assault: The threatened use of physical force or violence against another, that results in the person threatened being apprehensive of receiving an imminent battery (unlawful touching).

Aggravated Assault: The commission of an assault while armed with a dangerous or deadly weapon.

Battery: The actual intentional touching or striking of another person against the person's will.

> **Aggravated Battery:** Battery against another person using a deadly weapon, or causing bodily harm to that person.

Perhaps more simply put, an assault is threatening to unlawfully strike another, whereas battery is the actual unlawful, striking or touching of another. If either offense is committed while using a *weapon,* then the offense becomes either *aggravated assault* or *aggravated battery.* As a reminder, it is important to note that UCR data categorizes all assaults and batteries under the classification *aggravated assault.*

Introduction

The national trend in the United States is that aggravated assaults have been declining during the past 10 years as reported by law enforcement agencies from across the country. In 2003, the number of aggravated assaults reported in the United States was 857,921, which was a 3.8% decline from the number reported in 2002. The rate of aggravated assaults per 100,000 population dropped to 295, which was a decrease of 4.7% from the previous year. This equates to one aggravated assault every 35 seconds, nationally.

There are several important statistics to consider when discussing aggravated assaults. First of all, those cities with populations of 250,000 or more had an aggravated assault rate of 532 offenses per 100,000 population, which is significantly higher than the national average of 295 per 100,000 population. So it's clear that larger cities have more assaults than their smaller counterparts. It is also important to note that personal weapons, such as hands and feet, were used in 26.9% of aggravated assaults, while firearms were used in 19.1%, and knives in 18.2%. Other types of weapons (hammers, boards, etc.) were used in 35.9% of aggravated assaults reported in 2003.

In 2003, law enforcement agencies cleared 55.9% of reported aggravated assaults, and arrested about 450,000 individuals for committing the offense. Another important statistic when considering violent crime, is that arrests for aggravated assault equate to 75% of all violent crime arrests in the United

States. Of those persons arrested for aggravated assault in 2003, 86.3 were adults, with just under 14 percent being juveniles. Of those arrests 79.3% were male and 21.7% were female.

The following case is taken from the files of the Monroe County State Attorney's Office, Monroe County Sheriff's Office, and the Key West Police Department, all located in Key West, Florida.

Battery in the Tropics

September 2, 2000, was a typical sunny and humid day in Key West, Florida. The streets of the downtown area are narrow, and oftentimes cars are forced to pull over to one side to let other cars pass to avoid a collision. Cyclists and pedestrians are abundant in this tourist town known for its eccentric life style.

Craig Moore, a local who worked construction and performed other odd jobs around town, was riding his bicycle near South Street and Vernon. As Moore was approaching the intersection of these two streets, he noticed a black, late-model Ford pickup truck following very closely behind his bicycle. The driver of the pickup truck began honking his horn and motioning for Moore to get out of his way. As Moore continued toward the intersection, the pickup truck got even closer to the rear of Moore's bicycle, at which time Moore turned around and gestured to the Ford pickup truck driver to back off, and not follow so closely. The Ford pickup truck was driven by a white male, who, according to Moore, became increasingly agitated that Moore would not get out of his way. Several expletives were shouted back and forth between Moore and the pickup driver, when suddenly the driver of the truck jumped out of his vehicle and approached Moore, who was still straddling his bicycle. In the subsequent police reports that Moore would file concerning this incident, he described the driver of the pickup truck as a very muscular, white male in his 30s who was wearing a tank-top shirt.

As the driver of the pick-up truck approached Moore, he shouted at Moore, and then suddenly struck Moore with his fist, hitting Moore in the face. The force of the blow knocked Craig Moore from the bicycle causing his sunglasses to fly from his face. Both Moore and his bicycle hit the pavement, causing damage to the bicycle and abrasions on Moore's arms. Moore's sunglasses, which he had just recently purchased, were damaged beyond repair.

The Investigation

The driver of the pickup truck walked back to his vehicle and drove off. As the driver of the black pickup truck left the scene, Craig Moore noticed a police fraternal organization sticker on the truck's rear window, and another witness, Roger Schaal, was able to copy the license number of the truck as it departed.

When the Key West Police Department responded to the scene to investigate, Roger Schaal described the battery that occurred to Moore and provided the license plate number of the suspect's vehicle, along with a physical description of the perpetrator. Key West officers immediately conducted a vehicle registration check, utilizing the license number provided by Schaal, and determined that the vehicle belonged to Patrick Scribner, a Monroe County Sheriff's Deputy who lived in Key West. Once the Key West Police Department determined that a law enforcement officer may have committed the battery on Craig Moore, they contacted the Internal Affairs Division of the Monroe County Sheriff's Office, who then initiated an investigation on one of their own deputies.

In addition to the Sheriff's Internal Affairs, the Monroe County State Attorney's Investigative Unit also entered the case. After conducting victim and witness interviews and a photographic lineup, Deputy Patrick Scribner was positively identified. Scribner was officially charged with misdemeanor battery for striking Craig Moore in the face with his fist on September 2, 2000.

On May 5, 2001, Deputy Patrick Scribner entered into a Pre-Trial Intervention (PTI) agreement regarding the battery charge, and was subsequently placed on 6 months probation, assigned to 30 hours of community service, and was required to pay $153.00 in restitution. This allowed him to retain his Florida Law Enforcement certification, as his PTI agreement in this case would result in no criminal conviction after he successfully completed the required 6 month probation period.

Tragically, in the fall of 2003, Deputy Patrick Scribner was found dead in his home by an apparent self-inflicted gunshot wound, bringing an end to the life and career of this troubled officer.

You're the Investigator

1. Compare and contrast the offenses of assault and battery.

   _____

   _____

   _____

   _____

   _____

   _____

   _____

   _____

   _____

   _____

   _____

2. Identify the additional element necessary to make a simple assault and battery an aggravated assault and battery.

   _____

   _____

   _____

   _____

   _____

   _____

   _____

   _____

   _____

   _____

   _____

3. Describe the significance of aggravated assault on the over-all violent crime rate in the United States. Distinguish the aggravated assault rates between large and small communities.

_____

_____

_____

_____

_____

_____

_____

_____

_____

_____

_____

4. Describe and discuss elements of battery that existed when Scribner struck Moore.

_____

_____

_____

_____

_____

_____

_____

_____

_____

_____

_____

5. Describe the important evidence witnesses provided to investigators concerning the Moore battery.

_____

_____

_____

_____

_____

_____

_____

_____

_____

_____

6. Describe and discuss how investigators identified the suspect who committed the battery to Craig Moore.

_____

_____

_____

_____

_____

_____

_____

_____

_____

_____

_____

7. Describe the legal principle allowing defendant Patrick Scribner to avoid a criminal conviction on his record.

_____

_____

_____

_____

_____

_____

_____

_____

_____

_____

_____

8. Identify five reasons why you think individuals engage in assault and battery.

_____

_____

_____

_____

_____

_____

_____

_____

_____

_____

_____

_____

9. Describe the economic impact of assault and battery in today's society.

_____

_____

_____

_____

_____

_____

_____

_____

_____

_____

10. Describe the psychological and sociological impact of assault and battery in today's society.

_____

_____

_____

_____

_____

_____

_____

_____

_____

_____

_____

CHAPTER 5

Burglary

DEFINITION

According to the FBI's Uniform Crime Report, burglary is the entering of a building, or dwelling with intent to commit a crime therein. As an example, a burglar forcibly enters a home, and steals, or attempts to steal, the property of another. The unlawful entry with the intent to take property (theft) belonging to another person consummates the offense of burglary.

Introduction

In 2003, the United States had an estimated 2,153,464 burglaries, which was a slight increase (0.1%) over the previous year. This equates to a burglary occurring every 14.7 seconds, nationally. According to the FBI's Uniform Crime Report, there were 740 burglary offenses per 100,000 population in the United States. Collectively, victims of burglaries lost an estimated $3.5 billion, with an average loss of over $1,626 per incident.

Approximately 65% of all burglaries were residential, and most of these home burglaries (62%) occurred during the daytime hours. A further examination of burglary data reflects that 62% of burglaries involved *forcible entry* (breaking and entering), with 31% resulting from *unlawful entry* (entering unlocked premises, or remaining in premises after closing time). Additionally, attempted forcible entry constituted nearly 7% of all burglary offenses. Unfortunately, burglary is one of the offenses which law enforcement agencies have not enjoyed a great deal of success in solving. In 2003, only 13% of burglaries were cleared, nationally, by law enforcement.

Although burglary is considered a property crime, an element of danger and violence is present, particularly when a burglary occurs to an occupied dwelling, or when a resident or business owner returns home or to their business and interrupts a burglary in progress. Fortunately, homeowners are only present in about 10% of burglaries, but in those instances where that occurs there is a 30% chance the burglary victim may also become the victim of a violent crime.

Burglars much prefer to enter a house or business where no one is present, so they can quickly go about their business of stealing valuables, and getting away undetected. A burglar's primary motive is financial benefit, and one will usually sell the proceeds of the burglaries to a fence, (one who deals in stolen property) and receive only a small portion of the property's value. A burglar will generally use the same modus operandi, and it is not uncommon for burglars to work the same geographical area if they continue to be successful.

Burglary, like robbery, can be a difficult crime to solve. As previously noted, only 13% of burglaries are solved, and the difficulty in solving burglaries is in part due to the fact that successful burglars leave little or no evidence at the scene. In most instances, there are no eyewitnesses to identify the burglars.

In many jurisdictions, burglary to an occupied dwelling becomes a more serious offense and can become *home-invasion robbery,* depending on whether the actual or threatened use of physical force or violence is directed toward the occupants. The later offense, in many jurisdictions, is what is termed a non-probational offense, and carries a mandatory jail sentence.

Hollywood Art Caper

While a wealthy Hollywood movie producer and his family were out of town for the holidays, he asked the property manager for his huge Los Angeles estate to come by to check on the house periodically. During one early morning visit, the property manager noticed broken glass at the rear door of the mansion, and through subsequent checking, determined that over $400,000 in art was missing from the house. It was discovered that the items missing included Picasso's 1937 drawing *FAUNE*, and an expensive Tiffany lamp.

The subsequent police investigation determined that the broken glass was not actually the entry point into the house, but staged by the burglar to confuse the police and make them think the burglar had entered through the rear door. The police investigation determined that the glass was broken from the inside out. The forensic examination of the glass noted that the glass was laminated, which resulted in the glass fragments adhering to the laminated material, and causing the glass to bulge out, rather than bulge in. Investigators quickly determined that, based upon the physical evidence, the glass was broken from inside the house and forced out.

Additional evidence at the scene revealed muddy footprints coming from a side door into the billiard room. Further examination determined that there was no forced entry into the billiard room, and the muddy prints were due to a yard sprinkling system that came on about 4:00 a.m.

It was obvious to investigators that the burglary was an inside job, and the broken glass was a diversion. Determining who had access to the residence would not be easy, as nearly 30 full-time employees worked at the estate. These employees included maids, cooks, nannies, gardeners, personal assistants, chauffeurs, and others. Although the theft from the mansion was significant, the wealthy producer was more concerned about the safety and well-being of his family, realizing the perpetrator was likely someone that he was in contact with every day.

The Investigation

The stolen art was placed on the Los Angeles Police Department's (LAPD) Art Theft Detail website, and also put into various other art databases in hope that if someone attempted to sell the valuable art it would easily be recognized. For nearly five months the case remained unsolved and few leads developed. Then, a break occurred when a man, who said his name was Tony Hargain, came to the famed Christie's auction in Beverly Hills indicating that he was a professional football player, and had a real Picasso that he wanted to sell. The man claiming to be Hargain said he had purchased the drawing from a friend for $100,000. Although the man claimed not to have the artwork with him, he gave the Christie's employee he was talking with a detailed description of the artwork.

After listening to the customer's story, the Christie's employee, Nathalie, became suspicious, and excused herself under the pretext that she would need to research the artwork more thoroughly to determine its value. Instead, Nathalie checked a stolen art directory file, and learned that the piece in question had been stolen. Nathalie then immediately notified Christie's security personnel, who in turn contacted LAPD's Art Theft Detail. LAPD was concerned that if they arrived too quickly, the suspect might never tell authorities where the art was actually located, so a strategy was developed by the police to try to keep the suspect talking about the Picasso in hopes that the Christie's employee could learn its location, and perhaps to determine what kind of vehicle the suspect was driving, in case he became nervous and left before the police arrived.

Linda, the general manager of Christie's, agreed to the LAPD plan of action, and went to the lobby only to discover that the suspect, Tony Hargain, had left. Linda went out to the parking lot attempting to find Tony, and observed Tony ready to drive off in a BMW. Linda ran out to the street, and managed to talk Tony into coming back inside to continue to discuss the Picasso sale.

Once Tony came back inside Christie's, the conversation with Linda and Nathalie continued. Unbeknownst to Tony, Beverly Hills police officers were quickly and silently converging on Christie's. One officer entered through a rear door and began watching the suspect on a television monitor. Other officers took up surveillance positions watching the exits from the building and the suspect's BMW. Becoming more comfortable in his conversation with Linda and Nathalie, Tony mentioned that he also had several Picasso plates for sale (also stolen in the burglary). At that point, based on a predetermined signal from police, the Christie's employees told Tony that the "Picasso Expert" had just arrived, at which point Tony stated that he had the Picasso drawing in his car trunk. Tony then walked outside to his car, where he was observed removing a picture wrapped in a shirt. Tony brought the item into the store and unwrapped it, at which time the Christie's employees confirmed that it was the stolen Picasso.

By the time the LAPD's Art Theft Detail arrived, the suspect was already in custody and sitting handcuffed in Christie's lobby. LAPD detectives immediately recognized "Tony" as the movie producer's chauffeur, Sammie Archer III. From the beginning, Sammie was a prime suspect in the burglary, especially after he did not show up for a scheduled lie detector test. Archer was also a prime suspect in a defrauding of the movie producer out of $40,000 through a credit card scam. Archer came from a large family, and at least five of his brothers were serving time in state prison. Archer, who also had worked for comedian, Chevy Chase, was, up until now, the only one in the family without an arrest record. Archer's luck had run out!

Sammie Archer III was charged with burglary in the first degree, grand theft, embezzlement, and receiving stolen property. Archer's bond was set at $480,000.

When Archer was arrested, the other items taken in the burglary were not found in his vehicle. However, authorities obtained a search warrant for his residence where shoes were discovered that matched the muddy prints left at the scene. Authorities also found a handwritten list of other art and antique stores that Archer had contacted in an effort to sell the items.

Detectives were able to convince Archer to cooperate in the investigation, and he eventually provided the name of an antique dealer who, unknowingly, had purchased all of the remaining stolen items. This case clearly demonstrates the fluidity of the stolen art market. In less than 3 months, the expensive Tiffany lamp went through five separate purchases, and traveled across the country from Beverly Hills to New York, and then into Canada.

This case also demonstrates the unpredictable value in the art market. At the time of the theft, the Tiffany lamp was valued at $75,000 by a well-known appraiser. When police officers located the lamp, they determined it had been purchased for $275,000.

Sammie Archer III had gone through much of his adult life passing himself off as Tony Hargain, who happened to be a professional football player, and an acquaintance of Archer's when the two attended the University of Oregon. Both Hargain and Archer tried to become professional football players, but where Hargain succeeded, Archer failed. Nevertheless, Archer would use his friend's name to impress other people, even going so far as to tell his girlfriend, a model, that his name was Tony Hargain, and the luxury cars he drove as a chauffeur were his vehicles. Although Archer was not reluctant to use the identity of other people to orchestrate his crime career, an ironic and bizarre twist of fate occurred, when Archer encountered another inmate in the county jail who was wearing a wristband with the name "Sammie Archer III" on it. The other "Sammie Archer III" turned out to be one of Archer's brothers who had been using Sammie's name for years every time he was arrested.

Thanks to the alert employees at Christie's and the aggressive work of several police agencies, one of Los Angeles' most significant burglaries was solved, and nearly $500,000 in rare valuable art was recovered and returned to its owner.

You're the Investigator

1. List the elements of the offense of burglary identified in this case.

   _____

   _____

   _____

   _____

   _____

   _____

   _____

   _____

   _____

   _____

   _____

2. Describe and discuss why the art burglary was considered a property crime.

   _____

   _____

   _____

   _____

   _____

   _____

   _____

   _____

   _____

_____

_____

3. Describe the items of physical evidence existing at the crime scene that pointed toward the burglary being an inside job.

_____

_____

_____

_____

_____

_____

_____

_____

_____

_____

4. Describe the specific evidence found at the scene of the burglary linking the suspect, Archer, to the crime scene.

_____

_____

_____

_____

_____

_____

_____

_____

_____

_____

5. Analyze the forensic examination of the broken glass establishing that the glass was broken from inside the house not outside.

---

6. Describe investigators' efforts to alert art dealers of the theft so that if someone attempted to sell the art, dealers would be aware the items were stolen.

---

7. Discuss the concept of the value of art stolen and its impact on sentencing.

_____

_____

_____

_____

_____

_____

_____

_____

_____

_____

8. Describe the role of the Christie's employees in solving this case and recovering the stolen art.

_____

_____

_____

_____

_____

_____

_____

_____

_____

_____

9. Describe why art thieves are perceived to be more sophisticated than other criminals. Do you think perpetrators who steal art are any "smarter" than those who steal other merchandise?

_____

_____

_____

_____

_____

_____

_____

_____

_____

_____

_____

10. Identify five crime-prevention strategies to prevent art from being stolen.

_____

_____

_____

_____

_____

_____

_____

_____

_____

_____

_____

_____

CHAPTER 6

Larceny-Theft

DEFINITION

According to the FBI's Uniform Crime Report, larceny-theft is defined as the unlawful taking of property or cash of another with the intent to either temporarily or permanently deprive the owner of the property.

Introduction

The elements of the offense of *theft* vary from state to state, but generally involve *the taking of property of another without the owner's consent, with intent to either temporarily or permanently deprive the owner of the beneficial use of the property.* States also utilize different penalty structures for theft cases, and typically states determine the difference between *felony and misdemeanor theft* on the basis of the dollar value of the items that are taken in the theft. For example, in Florida, if the amount of the theft (stolen items) is more than $300 dollars, it is considered *felony theft* or *grand theft*. If the value of the stolen item(s) is less than $300 dollars, it is *misdemeanor* theft or *petit theft*. By classifying thefts in this manner, the penalty provisions assessed by the courts upon a defendant's conviction would be determined by the value of the stolen items. For purposes of the

Uniform Crime Report, *theft includes all items of any value unlawfully taken from the rightful owner.*

The UCR lists the following categories of offenses as *larceny-theft:*

- Purse snatching
- Pocket picking
- Bicycle theft
- Thefts from coin operated machines
- Thefts of motor vehicle parts
- Thefts from buildings
- Thefts from motor vehicles
- Shoplifting

Not included in the list of crimes that are considered larceny-theft in the UCR system are some of the traditional *white-collar crimes* such as *embezzlement, forgery, fraud,* and *bad checks.* Many criminologists believe that theft requires the actual physical possession of the items taken; whereas in many white-collar crimes, no actual item comes into the possession of the perpetrator. Instead, documents are falsified or created to defraud another of property or cash. These types of offenses are considered *Part II crimes* and are counted statistically in the UCR category.

It is also important to note that *auto theft* is its own Part I crime and is tracked separately from other theft cases in the UCR system.

Since both theft and robbery result in the taking of property or cash of another, what are the distinguishing characteristics of these crimes? *Theft is different from robbery in that thefts occur without personal contact with the owner of the property, while robbery occurs when property is taken from the person or in the presence of the owner through threatened or actual use of physical force or violence.*

Identity theft has become one of the greatest challenges to our modern criminal justice system. This new crime wave involves the theft of names, social security numbers, bank account information, credit card records, and other personal information which is either used by the thief or sold to other professional identity impersonators who will use the information to purchase cars, stereo equipment, visit pornography sites, and even take out mortgages while posing as the person whose identity is being fraudulently used. These types of thieves take little personal risk and often go undiscovered by law enforcement investigators. Both at the federal and state levels, specific legislation has been enacted to respond to the huge problem posed by identity theft. These new laws serve as useful tools for investigators who are responding to an alarming number of identity theft cases.

According to UCR data, there were 7,021,588 thefts reported by police agencies, nationally, in 2003. The value of the stolen property taken in these thefts was nearly $5 billion dollars. The theft of auto parts continues to be the most prevalent type of theft committed in the United States. Items such as radar detectors, wheels, tires, and other vehicle components appear to be the items of choice for thieves.

Larceny-theft continues to be the most commonly reported major crime in the United States, with a theft occurring every 4.5 seconds. Clearance rates for theft cases in 2003 were about 18%, with more than 735,000 individuals arrested during that period.

The Winona Ryder Shoplifting Case

On December 12, 2001, 31-year-old Oscar nominated actress, Winona Ryder, went on a shoplifting spree at the Saks Fifth Avenue store in Beverly Hills, California. Ryder, who starred in films such as *"The Age of Innocence," "Mr. Deeds," "Girl Interrupted,"* and *"Little Women,"* would spend several hours in the Saks store, during which time she purchased more than a thousand dollars worth of merchandise. However, by days end, Ryder would find herself arrested, and charged with shoplifting more than $5,000 worth of designer clothing, including an expensive Gucci dress worth more than $1,500, and several designer purses worth more than $500, along with a number of other expensive items.

According to authorities, during Ryder's shoplifting arrest, she was also found to have in her possession several different pain killers without an appropriate prescription.

Investigation

On December 12, 2001, Saks Fifth Avenue security personnel were monitoring surveillance cameras from a basement location in the exclusive store located on Wilshire Boulevard in Beverly Hills, California. The security investigators noticed an attractive woman, who they initially thought might be a homeless person due to her sloppy dress. The woman was observed carrying several shopping bags with a number of expensive items in her arm. As security officers continued to monitor the woman's actions, they observed her enter a dressing room with the items.

As security officers continued to focus the cameras on the dressing room where the woman had entered, they also advised the loss prevention investigator, Colleen Rainey, to respond to the area of the dressing room to observe the woman's actions. Upon Rainey's arrival, she looked through the slats of the dressing room door, and observed the woman on her knees using a pair of scissors to cut the sensor tags off the merchandise.

Continuing to watch the woman, Rainey observed her successfully remove security tags from a Dolce & Gabbana handbag, as well as a Natori purse. Rainey also watched the woman unsuccessfully attempt to get the sensors off of two additional purses. In the process, the woman appeared to cut her finger, and blood drops were observed on the purse.

As the woman emerged from the dressing room, security investigators noticed that the shopping bags she was carrying were significantly larger than when she entered the dressing room. As security continued to monitor the woman, they observed her attempt to hide the security tags that she had removed by placing them in the pocket of a Gucci coat that was hanging on a rack. The woman also appeared to hide the security tags in other locations in the store according to investigators. Investigators seized these tags as evidence, as several of them had cloth from the stolen items still attached to the sensors.

Saks security personnel continued to conduct surveillance on the woman as she struggled to control the heavy shopping bags. At one point, due to the weight of the items, the woman actually fell, losing control of her items. After picking up her bags, the woman struggled to the store exit. As she attempted to leave the store without paying for the merchandise, she was stopped by several security officers. As security officers confronted the woman, they noticed that a hat which she had worn into the dressing room, and had taken from another floor of the department store, was now in one of the shopping bags. As security officers questioned the poverty-stricken-looking woman whom they had initially thought was a homeless person, they were surprised to learn that they had caught one of Hollywood's better-known female stars Winona Ryder, shoplifting.

When confronted by Saks security personnel about the merchandise in her possession, Ryder initially stated, "My director directed me to shoplift for a role." Ryder also attempted to have security let her charge the items to her credit card that she alleged the store had on file to accommodate "celebrity shoppers." A quick check by security confirmed that Ryder was not registered for the program that Saks offered to some of Hollywood's elite. Ryder was detained by Saks security personnel until police arrived. She was subsequently arrested and charged with four counts of Grand Theft and Possession of Controlled Substances under California law.

The Trial

Winona Ryder's trial began on October 24, 2002. Ryder was represented by famous defense attorney, Mark Geragos, a well-known lawyer in the Los Angeles area.

During the prosecutor's presentation of its case, various video tapes were played showing Ryder in possession of merchandise with tags entering a dressing room, and then exiting with the items stuffed into various shopping bags. The prosecution also presented the testimony of Saks security investigators who observed Ryder cutting security tags off the merchandise in the dressing room, as well as testimony that she was observed hiding the security devices in various areas of the store. Prosecutors also attempted to introduce evidence of several "prior bad acts," video tapes of Ryder during an alleged shoplifting that occurred at Barneys in New York, and one at Neiman Marcus in Beverly Hills. Although Ryder was not charged in these two incidents, the prosecutors contended that the videos demonstrated that Ryder had engaged in this same behavior on previous occasions.

Ryder's attorney argued in a closed hearing before Superior Court Judge Eldon Fox, that the jury should not be permitted to view the video tape evidence of the previous alleged shoplifting instances, as Ryder was not detained or charged in those instances. Judge Fox ultimately ruled that jurors would not be permitted to view the other incidents, as the evidence would impair Ryder's ability to have a fair trial.

After the prosecution concluded its case, the defense strategy was to demonstrate that the video tapes never actually showed Ryder concealing any items; nor did they show that she removed any security tags. Ryder's lawyer argued that Ryder gave her credit card to an employee of Saks when she first entered the store and the employee agreed to keep her account open while she shopped.

In December of 2002, Judge Fox sentenced Ryder to three years probation, 480 hours of community service, $10,000 in restitution and fines, and Ryder was ordered to undergo drug and psychiatric counseling.

You're the Investigator

1. Identify the legal elements of the crime of theft.

   _____

   _____

   _____

   _____

   _____

   _____

   _____

   _____

   _____

   _____

   _____

2. Discuss how the severity of a theft case is impacted by the value of the property stolen.

   _____

   _____

   _____

   _____

   _____

   _____

   _____

   _____

   _____

   _____

   _____

3. Compare and contrast the crimes of theft and robbery.

_____

_____

_____

_____

_____

_____

_____

_____

_____

_____

4. Describe the investigative techniques used by loss-prevention investigators at Saks Fifth Avenue to catch Ryder committing shoplifting. Why did they become suspicious of Ryder?

_____

_____

_____

_____

_____

_____

_____

_____

_____

_____

5. Describe the evidence on which investigators and prosecutors charged Winona Ryder with grand theft.

_____

_____

_____

_____

_____

_____

_____

_____

_____

_____

_____

6. Discuss the defense strategy used at Ryder's trial to prove
   that she did not commit theft from the Saks department store.

_____

_____

_____

_____

_____

_____

_____

_____

_____

_____

7. Describe the prosecutor's motivation for wanting to introduce
   evidence of Ryder's previous alleged shoplifting episodes.

_____

_____

_____

_____

_____

_____

_____

_____

_____

_____

_____

8. Discuss why Judge Fox refused to admit videotapes of prior instances of "bad acts" by Winona Ryder.

_____

_____

_____

_____

_____

_____

_____

_____

_____

9. Why do you think Ryder would shoplift when she can afford to pay for the merchandise?

_____

_____

_____

_____

_____

_____

_____

_____

_____

_____

_____

10. Do you think celebrities who shoplift should be treated more harshly, more leniently, or the same as the general public?

_____

_____

_____

_____

_____

_____

_____

_____

_____

_____

_____

CHAPTER 7

Motor Vehicle Theft

DEFINITION

According to the FBI's Uniform Crime Report, motor vehicle theft is defined as the taking of a motor vehicle without the consent of the owner. A motor vehicle is defined as a self propelled vehicle that runs on the ground and not on rails.

Introduction

Examples of motor vehicles include automobiles, motorcycles, trucks, buses, motor scooters, and snowmobiles. Excluded in the UCR definition are airplanes, boats, trains, construction, and farm equipment to include bulldozers and tractors. The unlawful taking of these items would be considered a larceny as opposed to motor vehicle theft.

According to the FBI and Insurance Information Institute, motor vehicle theft is on the rise in the United States. After a nearly 10 year decline in motor vehicle theft rates, an increase in thefts began in 1999 and has risen 9.4% in the period 1999–2003. A motor vehicle theft occurs every 25.3 seconds, nationally.

According to 2003 FBI data, the following is indicative of the U.S. motor vehicle theft problem:

There were 1,260,471 motor vehicle thefts in 2003.

The value of vehicles stolen in 2003 in the United States exceeded 8 billion dollars.

The average loss per stolen vehicle in 2003 was $7,100.

In 2003, the odds of a vehicle being stolen in the United States were 1 in 186.

Over two-thirds of all motor vehicle thefts occur at night.

Only 13.1% of motor vehicle thefts were cleared by arrests in 2003.

The recovery rate for stolen motor vehicles was 63%.

In the United States 63.8% of vehicle theft arrests involve individuals who are under 25 years of age, and 30.4% arrested are under 18 years of age.

Carjacking accounts for 3% of all motor vehicle thefts nationwide.

The two days with the highest number of recorded motor vehicle thefts are Friday and Saturday.

Western states have experienced the greatest increase (5.7%) in motor vehicle theft cases.

In 2003, according to the National Insurance Crime Bureau (NICB), the following metropolitan areas were ranked as the "top ten" for motor vehicle theft in the United States.

Rank	Metropolitan Area	Vehicles Stolen	Rate[1]
1	Modesto, CA	6,016	1,345.87
2	Phoenix, AZ	40,769	1,253.71
3	Stockton, CA	6,730	1,194.11
4	Las Vegas, NV	18,103	1,158.01
5	Sacramento, CA	17,054	1,047.42
6	Fresno, CA	9,102	986.65
7	Oakland, CA	23,199	969.63
8	Miami, FL	21,088	935.85
9	San Diego, CA	26,091	927.24
10	Detroit, MI	40,197	905.02

[1]Rate is the number of vehicle thefts reported per 100,000 people based on the 2000 census.

Motor vehicle thefts can occur for a variety of reasons, and therefore fall into the following categories:

Joy-ride A vehicle is taken, generally by a youthful offender, and is driven around for transportation purposes, and then left on the street where, generally, the vehicles are recovered by law enforcement and returned to the owner.

Insurance fraud This occurs when the vehicle owner is attempting to dispose of the vehicle and collect insurance. In many instances, vehicles are falsely reported stolen by the owner, and the vehicles are burned, hidden, or provided to professional car thieves who will dispose of the vehicle. The owner then contacts police and the insurance company reporting the vehicle missing with the intent of collecting insurance payment for the value of the vehicle.

Professional car thief This occurs when an individual, but more likely a group or gang, steals vehicles for the purpose of taking parts from the vehicles, and selling the parts. These operations are commonly referred to as *chop shops,* which usually are garages or warehouses where the thieves bring the vehicles. The thieves very quickly disassemble the vehicles, and then sell the parts or build new vehicles by combining parts from various vehicles they have stolen. In these cases, thieves may alter the vehicle identification numbers (VINs) which appear on various parts of the vehicle, so as to conceal the fact that the vehicle or parts are stolen.

Also, these professional vehicle thieves who live near a border or port area may steal vehicles for the purpose of shipping them out of the country, where certain types of luxury cars may be sold for nearly twice their U.S. value.

Steal car to commit another crime—This occurs when a vehicle has been stolen and is used in the commission of another crime. Frequently, bank robbers and other criminals will steal a vehicle to use in the commission of a robbery, to avoid using their own vehicle which could easily be traced to them through the vehicle's license plate.

Motor Vehicle Theft has become one of the most significant financial crimes in the United States, with the value of motor vehicle thefts exceeding 8.6 billion dollars in 2003. A recent trend for car thieves is to steal airbags and xenon high intensity head-lights. Last year, more than 100,000 air bags were stolen from vehicles. Costs can run between $500–$2,000 for a dealer to install replacement airbags. Auto thieves can steal airbags in less than 3 minutes and then sell them for $25–$50 dollars to mechanics who will then advertise airbag installation at a fraction of the dealer installed costs. Of course, the other implication is that if the theft is covered by insurance, these "shady mechanics" will bill the insurance company a much higher price than that for which they purchased the airbags on the "black market." Similarly, xenon high-intensity headlights, which can cost in excess of $2,000 to install on a vehicle, have become the target of car thieves. Stolen lights can result in a significant profit in the lucrative specialty car market.

There is an aspect of motor vehicle crime that can be very dangerous and violent, and that is *carjacking*. *Carjacking is the taking of a motor vehicle from the person of another or from the custody of another, and in the course of the larceny of the vehicle there is the use of force, violence, assault, or putting another in fear.* Carjacking has received national attention in recent times due to the violent nature of the crime and the fact that sometimes victims are taken hostage by the carjacker. Fortunately, according to 2003 FBI data, carjacking accounts for only about 3% of all motor vehicle thefts.

It is interesting to note that, based upon national arrest data, 63% of motor vehicle thefts are committed by young males under 25 years of age, and more than 83% of all motor vehicle thefts are committed by male offenders.

Grand Theft Auto

The typical auto-theft case occurs when the perpetrator identifies the geographical area in which to commit the theft, and has predetermined the type of vehicle that has been targeted. The vehicle is broken into, the ignition punched, the car "hot wired," and then driven off by the thief.

The Anthony Beeks/Wendell DeVaughn Martin case, however, is a much more complex criminal case in which fraud schemes were utilized to steal a number of cars and motorcycles valued at more than $130,000 dollars.

The location was Jacksonville, Florida, and it was the early Summer of 2000, when Special Agent Vecchio of the Florida Department of Law Enforcement received information that a criminal enterprise was being operated by Wendell DeVaughn Martin. Specifically, Special Agent Vecchio learned that Martin and several cohorts were engaged in an organized scheme to commit grand theft of motor vehicles.

Special Agent Vecchio, working with Special Agent Tracy Cunningham of the FBI, and Sgt. Urana Harris of the Florida Highway Patrol (FHP), developed confidential informant information that ABC Car Consultants of Jacksonville, Florida, was engaged in the business of charging fees to "clients" in exchange for arranging loans for the clients to purchase motor vehicles, which were obtained through local Jacksonville car dealerships. It was further determined by investigators that ABC Car Consultants frequently obtained loans for the purchase of these vehicles from various financial institutions by utilizing stolen social security numbers, fraudulent payroll invoices, and other false information to service the loans. The owner of ABC Car Consultants was Anthony Conrad Beeks, and his financial consultant was Wendell DeVaughn Martin, who worked as a freelance loan facilitator for ABC Car Consultants.

As investigators proceeded with their investigation, they learned that on June 3, 2000, Martin appeared at Ron Turner Cycles, located at 10263 Beach Blvd. in Jacksonville, Florida, with a person who identifed herself as Camille Glover, and two unidentified male subjects. Wendell Martin assisted Camille

Glover in the purchase and loan processing of two new Suzuki motorcycles valued at a total of nearly $23,000 dollars. The purchase of the motorcycles was arranged by Wendell Martin, who obtained financing for Camille Glover through Trans America Retail Financial Service, located in Shawnee Mission, Kansas.

In arranging the financing, Wendell Martin indicated that he represented ABC Car Consultants, and during the loan application process for Camille Glover, a willing participant, provided false personal information. The information included: false employment and salary data, including a fraudulent computer generated payroll account invoice, false address information, and a phony social security number for Glover. All of this information was provided to justify Glover's loan, even though none of the information was true. Special Agent Vecchio later learned that Anthony Beeks, the owner of ABC Car Consultants, gave the fictitious payroll account invoices to Wendell Martin to demonstrate that Glover was indeed employed. These phony payroll documents helped secure the loan authorization for Glover. By providing the false documentation, the loan was authorized by Trans America Retail Financial Service, and Martin, Glover, and the two unidentified males were permitted to leave Ron Turner Cycles with the two new Suzuki Motorcycles. The Martin, Beeks, Glover conspiracy had been successful in defrauding Trans America Retail Financial Service and Ron Turner Cycles out motorcycles worth nearly $23,000.

Based upon confidential informant information provided to investigators, it was determined that Camille Glover was not the intended recipient of the motorcycles. Although the motorcycles have not been recovered, it is believed they were taken to South Florida and sold.

The Investigation

On June 10, 2000, Special Agent Vecchio learned that Wendell Martin purchased two more new Suzuki motorcycles from Ron Turner Cycles using a similar scheme. Only this time Martin altered a counterfeit check as a down payment on the motorcycles. Once again, Martin provided fictitious identification and false personal information to Trans America Retail Financial Services, who again provided the loan to purchase the $23,000 worth of motorcycles. Martin's scheme worked again, and he was able to leave Ron Turner's Cycles with two new Suzuki motorcycles valued at nearly $23,000 dollars.

As Special Agent Vecchio's investigation progressed, he learned that on June 22, 2000, Richard Williams purchased a 2001 Ford F-150 pickup truck valued at $33,210 dollars from Mike Davidson Ford in Jacksonville. Investigators also learned that Wendell Martin aided in the transaction and worked in concert with Richard Williams to purposefully and intentionally provide false information, including a phony date of birth, social security number, address, and phone number, along with fictitious employment and salary information to Ford Motor Credit Corporation to authorize and approve a loan for the vehicle. Martin's and William's actions enabled them to leave the premises of Mike Davidson Ford with the new F-150 pickup truck. Richard C. Williams was subsequently arrested by the Florida Highway Patrol and the stolen vehicle was recovered.

Wendell Martin repeated his scheme on July 8, 2000, when he worked in concert with Adrian Williams to purchase a $30,000 dollar Ford Expedition by, once again, providing false and fictitious information to obtain a loan for the vehicle. This time the victims were Fidelity National Bank and Morrison Pontiac of Jacksonville.

Again, on July 18, 2000, a person identifying himself as Wendell Martin contacted Westside Toyota of Jacksonville, and represented himself as an associate of Rhonda Hightower, a/k/a Rhonda Robinson, and intentionally provided fraudulent information to the dealership so that Hightower could obtain a loan for a $30,000, 2000 model Toyota Avalon. The fraudulent information enabled Martin and Hightower to remove the Toyota from the premises of Westside Toyota.

As a result of the Beeks-Martin investigation, investigators were able to arrest Anthony Beeks, Wendell Martin, and Rhonda Hightower, a/k/a Robinson, for obtaining nearly $200,000 worth of motor vehicles through false and fraudulent pretenses.

Anthony Beeks, the ringleader of the group, was sentenced in Federal Court in Jacksonville, Florida, on May 18, 2005, to 51 months in federal prison, and was ordered to pay restitution in the amount of $179,000 dollars to the various victims. Wendell Martin was sentenced on state charges to one year and six months in state prison, and Rhonda Hightower, a/k/a Robinson, was given one year probation for her participation in the motor vehicle thefts.

You're the Investigator

1. Describe and discuss the elements of motor vehicle theft.

   _____

   _____

   _____

   _____

   _____

   _____

   _____

   _____

   _____

   _____

2. Analyze the current motor vehicle theft trends in the United States.

   _____

   _____

   _____

   _____

   _____

   _____

   _____

   _____

   _____

   _____

3. Describe four categories of motor vehicle theft committed by car thieves. What was the thieves' intent in each category?

_____

_____

_____

_____

_____

_____

_____

_____

_____

_____

4. Discuss why carjacking is the most dangerous form of motor vehicle theft.

_____

_____

_____

_____

_____

_____

_____

_____

_____

_____

5. Compare and contrast the "modus operandi" in the Beeks-Martin auto-theft ring to the more typical motor vehicle theft.

_____

_____

_____

_____

_____

_____

_____

_____

_____

_____

6. Describe the scheme utilized by Beeks-Martin to commit the motor vehicle thefts.

_____

_____

_____

_____

_____

_____

_____

_____

_____

7. Discuss the investigative techniques and sources of information that helped investigators solve the Beeks-Martin motor vehicle theft ring.

_____

_____

_____

_____

_____

_____

_____

_____

_____

8. List five reasons why individuals engage in motor vehicle theft.

_____

_____

_____

_____

_____

_____

_____

_____

_____

9. Identify and discuss five prevention strategies for curtailing motor vehicle theft.

_____

_____

_____

_____

_____

_____

_____

_____

_____

10. Discuss whether the punishment fits the crime in this case.

_____

_____

_____

CHAPTER 8

Arson

DEFINITION

According to the FBI's Uniform Crime Report, arson is generally considered to be the intentional and unlawful burning or attempted burning of property, whether with or without the intent to defraud.

Introduction

According to 2003 Uniform Crime Report data, there were more than 71,000 arson offenses reported to law enforcement agencies throughout the United States. This equates to one arson occurring every 7 minutes, nationally. Of these 71,000 arsons that were reported to law enforcement agencies, the estimated dollar loss exceeded $11,940 per offense. There were 16,163 people arrested for arson in 2003, and 84% of those arrested were males, with more than 50% of the arson arrestees under the age of 18, and 31% of those arrested less than 15 years of age.

The dollar amount of loss for residential arsons averaged more than $19,000 for single family dwellings, and more than $23,900 for multiple family residences. The lowest dollar loss for residential arsons was for mobile homes, which averaged more than $6,300 per arson.

U.S. law enforcement agencies solved 16.7% of reported arsons during 2003; juvenile offenders comprised over 41% of the cleared cases.

Arson is the act of deliberately setting fire to property for malicious or fraudulent purposes. It is a crime in all 50 states. In 2003, arson's total cost to our society was more than 1.5 billion, with vandalism being the leading cause of arson in the United States. It has been estimated that more than 475 people died in the United States, directly related to arson, and more than 2000 sustained injuries.

Motives for committing arson vary, and often involve either *direct* or *indirect financial gain,* such as the case when arson is committed to defraud an insurance company. *Revenge and concealment of another crime* are also significant reasons for committing arsons. In the case of juveniles, arson is often committed to *have fun or relieve boredom.* Another prominent motive in arsons results from the emotionally unbalanced individual who gets high from setting fires and watching a structure burn.

Unlike some other crimes, arson is usually difficult to identify, because the fire itself often destroys the evidence of the crime. Generally speaking, arsonists are law-abiding and don't have criminal pasts. The tools that an arsonist needs to commit the crime are common and ordinary for people to have in their possession, such as matches, lighters, etc., and these items can legally be carried on the person. This minimum risk is in stark contrast to the armed robber, who may use a deadly weapon that he or she is not authorized to possess, and then also runs the risk of getting caught with money or other evidence taken during the crime.

The Seaton Hall University Arson

On January 19, 2000, Seaton Hall University, in South Orange, New Jersey, became the site of one of the most horrific and deadly dormitory fires in American higher education history.

That year the freshman class had become accustomed to being awakened in the middle of the night by the fire alarm, which was frequently set off as a prank by some of the students living in the dormitory. It was not uncommon for the alarm to be activated several times a night, and it became so aggravating that residents soon began to ignore the obnoxious noise that radiated throughout the concrete block hallways of Boland Hall, which was one of the larger dormitories on the Seaton Hall campus.

During the evening hours of January 19, 2000, freshmen Tom Pugliese and Frank Caltabilota, were once again awakened by the sound of the fire alarm, only this time something was different. Both roommates looked toward their door and observed very heavy dark smoke invading their room at the bottom of the door.

Even though there had been frequent false alarms, no one had instructed the students as to what they should do in case of a real fire. Actually, there had never been a fire evacuation drill conducted, nor were there any sprinklers in the rooms that could be activated in case of a fire.

By now, the smoke was beginning to permeate the room, and Tom Pugliese and Frank Caltabilota realized they must act quickly. The door to their room was extremely hot to the touch, but both boys decided it wasn't safe to attempt to jump from the window of their room to the ground below, a forty foot drop. So Frank dropped to the floor and began crawling out into the hallway where he encountered heavy swirling smoke and dangerous fumes. As Frank crawled past the door's threshold, he turned left, and Tom later testified that that was the last time he saw Frank.

Investigators later determined that it was probable that Frank was dead shortly after he crawled from his room into the hallway. The young freshman would be one of three students to perish in the deadly Seaton Hall fire. Fortunately for Tom Pugliese, he turned right as he crawled into the hallway, and although he sustained significant burns and smoke inhalation, he was able to get out of the building.

In an another hallway of the building, a 21-year-old resident assistant for the building, Dana Christmas, made a difficult decision, to remain in the building to help other students instead of fleeing the building to safety. Through the heavy choking smoke, Dana went room to room, knocked on doors, and attempted to alert other students of the danger. During her effort to save others, Dana suffered severe burns to her hands and head as the intensity of the heat from the fire caused her hair to ignite. Dana ultimately passed out and was carried out of the building by another student.

At the other end of Boland Hall, student Nick Donato became disoriented in the smoke-filled hallway, and somehow was able to return to his room, where he realized he was trapped. With no other option remaining, Nick kicked out the window of his dorm room, and then crawled through the jagged glass and hung from the window sill by his hands. Nick clung to the window as long as he could, and then pushed off the building with his feet and fell to the ground below. After he landed, Nick tried to get up, and only then did he realize that he had broken his left foot, wrist, and a bone in his back in the nearly three story fall from his dormitory room. Nick looked up at the smoke billowing from his room, and, although in tremendous pain, he realized that he survived.

Clearly, a fire of this magnitude resulted in a tremendous response from the fire department, police agencies, and the media. As students fled the dorm, congregated, and watched firefighters attempt to contain the fire, television and newspaper reporters interviewed students to get their stories. A student named Joe LaPore, who seemed unnerved by the disaster, got out of the building without injury as did his roommate, and childhood friend, Sean Ryan. Although Ryan did not stop to talk to reporters, LaPore was more than willing to discuss his experience.

It was not long after LaPore's comments to the media, that federal arson investigators for the Bureau of Alcohol, Tobacco, and Firearms (BATF) determined that the fire didn't result from faulty electrical wiring, or even a student falling asleep with a cigarette. They came to the conclusion that this deadly blaze that took three young lives had been deliberately set. Investigators focused on Sean Ryan and Joe LaPore as the cause of the deadly blaze at Boland Hall.

The Investigation

The investigative team that worked together on this case consisted of experienced arson investigators from BATF, New Jersey State Police, and local police agencies. A number of these officers had worked complex cases in the past, including the 1993 World Trade Center bombing, and the Unabomber case.

Because of the experience level of the officers assigned to the Seaton Hall University fire, they quickly realized this was a difficult and complex case, as arson cases generally are. Unlike other criminal investigations, arson cases frequently result in limited physical evidence that can be linked to the perpetrator, because the intensity of the fire often destroys or seriously alters those items.

Investigators quickly determined that no accelerant was used in the fire, based upon burn patterns that were discovered on the lounge floor, where they determined the fire started. Authorities also learned that on January 21, two days after the fire, LaPore, Ryan, and two of their close friends, Santino "Tino" Cataldo and Mike Karpenski, met in their hometown of Fordham Park, New Jersey. During the meeting at a local donut shop, they discussed some of the events surrounding the fire.

Authorities knew that all four of the friends were present that night at Boland Hall, and they also knew, from a video camera, that Cataldo and Karpenski had left the dorm about an hour before the fire started. Grand Jury testimony established that Cataldo and Karpenski were also present at the dorm when Sean Ryan tore down a paper banner that a resident manager, Dan Nugent, put up to welcome students returning from Christmas break.

The investigation caused authorities to believe the fire may have started with the banner. Those suspicions were confirmed when several witnesses, including Dan Nugent, provided statements indicating they had observed the banner ablaze on one of the couches in the lounge. Nugent told police he used a phone to call in the fire, and he tried putting the fire out with a fire extinguisher, but due to the excitement, could only break one seal on the extinguisher. Nugent also advised authorities that there were previous incidents where paper signs were torn down and set on fire in the lounge. Additionally, many of the students knew there was bad blood between Nugent and the students from Fordham Park, because Nugent initiated disciplinary action against Ryan and LaPore when he smelled marijuana in their room.

Authorities learned that at the donut shop meeting, the four boys from Fordham Park agreed they would never disclose any information about the banner.

Shortly after the donut shop meeting, the conspiracy fell apart. During Sean Ryan's interview with authorities, he finally admitted that he pulled the banner off the wall, but steadfastly denied having any knowledge about how the fire started. When pressed during the interview by investigators, Ryan stated, "I'm no rat." He refused to provide further information. Investigators served over 100 grand jury subpoenas to friends of LaPore and Ryan, as well as other witnesses, and slowly an image of what transpired that deadly night developed.

Although grand jury proceedings are required by law to remain secret, events from the nearly four-year long probe and trial began to emerge, and eventually the investigation concluded that the fire began as a fraternity prank and got out of control. Authorities learned that Sean Ryan and another fraternity member began wrestling in the lounge at Boland Hall. During the wrestling match, Nugent, the resident manager, came to the lounge due to the loud noise, and made everybody leave the lounge.

The next key piece of evidence evolved when another freshman, Gabe Smith, whose room was next to LaPore and Ryan's room, provided testimony to the grand jury that he and his roommate, John Giunta, who died as a result of the fire, were talking in their room minutes before the fire started, and they heard footsteps leaving LaPore's and Ryan's room. According to information given to law enforcement, Smith heard the footsteps moving toward the stairway at the opposite end of the hallway from the lounge. Shortly after that, Smith said he heard the alarm go off. This proved to be vital information, because LaPore had previously given a statement to reporters that he was in his room when the alarm went off and initially thought it was another false alarm.

Additional aspects of the conspiracy unraveled when Karpenski, who initially testified before the grand jury that he had no knowledge of the fire, at the advice of his attorney, changed his story and admitted knowledge of the fire. Karpenski also testified about the donut shop meeting in Fordham Park, and that the participants agreed not to discuss the banner.

Authorities now had several critical components for their case. They had a motive for the crime, the feud between the Fordham Park boys and Nugent, the resident manager of the dorm. With Karpenski's testimony, authorities demonstrated that a conspiracy existed to withhold information, and the boys had the opportunity to commit the crime. But the one important piece of evidence authorities lacked was who actually ignited the banner.

Investigators continued to put pressure on Ryan and LaPore, but it was clear their attorneys would not let the boys talk. Investigators had another option. A mob "hitman," named Tom Ricciardi, was cooperating with law enforcement authorities on a variety of cases, attempting to get his prison sentence shortened. It turned out that Ricciardi had a brother named Daniel "Bobo" Ricciardi, who was friendly with Joe LaPore's mother. Through this relationship, Tom Ricciardi's brother was able to secure enough information and probable cause for authorities to get warrants to tap phones in LaPore's residence, as well as Ryan's cell phone. For nearly two years, authorities wiretapped calls at the LaPore residence, and on Ryan's cell phone and during that time period were able to collect valuable evidence that resulted in LaPore's father, sister, and mother being charged with obstruction of justice. Based upon the language in the indictment, the family members talked about the case on nine occasions, and during one conversation, LaPore's father discussed moving the family out of town before his son, Joe LaPore, could be charged. Also, authorities had recorded statements of LaPore's mother urging family members to lie to investigators, and "stay united."

Perhaps the most important information authorities obtained in the wiretaps was a statement Joe LaPore made to his sister, which, according to transcripts of the conversation was, "I didn't think I set the fire." Moments later, he stated, "I set it, I set it!"

In May of 2003, Seaton Hall University conducted its commencement exercises. Among those graduating were many of the survivors of the Boland Hall fire of more than three years before. To honor those who perished in the fire, the names of Aaron Karol, John Giunta, and Frank Caltabilota were placed on a diploma in their memory.

Nearly three weeks after the graduation, and almost three and one half years after the tragic Seaton Hall University fire that left three students dead and many injured, authorities released a 60 count indictment charging Joe LaPore and Sean Ryan with arson, reckless manslaughter, and felony murder. If convicted of these charges both Ryan and LaPore could be sentenced to life in prison. Additionally, indictments charged Cataldo, and LaPore's mother, sister, and father with obstruction of justice, carrying punishment of up to five years in prison.

At the time of writing, the Seaton Hall University arson case was still on the trial docket in Essex County, New Jersey, and was expected to go to trial by the summer of 2006.

An interesting project for class is to research and review the sentencing of Ryan, LaPore, Cataldo, and LaPore's mother, sister, and father when a disposition is rendered.

You're the Investigator

1. Describe and discuss the elements of the crime of arson established in this case.

   _____

   _____

   _____

   _____

   _____

   _____

   _____

   _____

   _____

   _____

   _____

   _____

2. Analyze why students were slow to respond to the fire alarm at Boland Hall.

   _____

   _____

   _____

   _____

   _____

   _____

   _____

   _____

   _____

   _____

   _____

_____

_____

3. Why are arson cases more difficult to solve than other crimes?

_____

_____

_____

_____

_____

_____

_____

_____

_____

_____

4. Describe how investigators determined that the fire began in the student lounge.

_____

_____

_____

_____

_____

_____

_____

_____

_____

_____

5. Discuss the evidence investigators discovered that established a motive for the Seaton Hall University arson.

_____

_____

_____

_____

_____

_____

_____

_____

_____

_____

_____

6. Describe the elements of conspiracy that authorities identified resulting from the donut shop meeting between the Fordham Park boys.

_____

_____

_____

_____

_____

_____

_____

_____

_____

_____

_____

7. Identify the critical evidence authorities obtained through the wiretap on the LaPore family home.

_____

_____

_____

_____

_____

_____

_____

_____

_____

_____

_____

8. Identify and discuss five reasons why individuals commit arson.

_____

_____

_____

_____

_____

_____

_____

_____

_____

_____

9. If you were the sentencing judge for the family member who obstructed justice, what penalty would you impose and why?

_____

_____

_____

_____

_____

_____

_____

_____

_____

_____

_____

10. If you were the sentencing judge for Ryan and LaPore, what
penalty would you impose?

_____

_____

_____

_____

_____

_____

_____

_____

_____

_____

_____